MARCH

OF

THE

GODS

OTHER BOOKS BY GARY JENNINGS

FOR YOUNG ADULTS
March of the Heroes
March of the Robots
The Rope in the Jungle (novel)
The Teenager's Realistic Guide to Astrology
The Shrinking Outdoors
Black Magic, White Magic
The Killer Storms
Parades!
The Movie Book

FOR PRESCHOOL READERS
The Earth Book

FOR ADULTS
Sow the Seeds of Hemp (novel)
The Terrible Teague Bunch (novel)
The Treasure of the Superstition Mountains
Personalities of Language

MARCH

OF

THE

GODS

GARY
JENNINGS

Drawings by
Dan Culhane

**ASSOCIATION
PRESS**

NEW YORK

MARCH OF THE GODS

Copyright © 1976 by Gary Jennings

Published by Association Press, 291 Broadway, New York, N.Y. 10007

International Standard Book Number: 0-8096-1912-1
Library of Congress Catalog Card Number: 76–8832

Library of Congress Cataloging in Publication

Jennings, Gary.
    March of the gods.

    Includes index.
    1. Gods—Juvenile literature. 2. God—Comparative studies—Juvenile literature. 3. Religion—Juvenile literature. I. Title.
BL473.J46   291.2'11   76–8832
ISBN 0–8096–1912–1

Printed in the United States of America
Designed by The Etheredges

FOR SHERYL

En ciel un dieu,
Par terre une déesse . . .

CONTENTS

God's First Commandment to the Israelites was,
"Thou shalt have none other gods . . ."
He did not say,
"There are no other gods!"

AUTHOR'S

NOTE

It is customary, in books addressed to English-language readers, to refer to that deity worshipped by most of the English-speaking world as "God" with a capital G, and to use reverently capitalized pronouns when speaking of "Him." Other languages do not capitalize the name of this deity (French *dieu*, Spanish *dios*, and so on), and it is possible that this book will be read by at least a few persons who worship some other deity. Therefore, throughout these pages, I have used the capitalized "God" when speaking of any divinity who is the one and only deity of any religion (Jehovah, Allah, *et al.*); I have used "god" with a small g when speaking of any of the many deities of those cultures which recognize and worship more than one (ancient Egypt, modern India, *et al.*); and I have not capitalized pronouns referring to any God or gods.

To avoid controversy, I have tried as hard as possible in this book to avoid overmuch discussion or comparison of the world's diverse *religions,* and have tried to concentrate on their *gods* (and goddesses and devils and demons). It is obvious, however, that no god could exist without a body of worshippers, and that no religion could exist without something to worship. Thus it has often been necessary for me to give at least a sketchy account of this or that religion in order to explain the motive of various peoples for adopting the god they did, the god's relation to those peoples and their ways of life, the similarities or differences between one set of gods and another, and so on. I hope that my reader, of whatever faith, will find that I have treated his or her religion impartially and fairly, just as I have tried to treat all the others.

Not at all incidentally, let me here express my gratitude to Mr. Frederick Schilz, who illuminated and enlivened many aspects of this book by generously sharing with me his fund of theological knowledge—and to my publisher/editor Mr. Robert W. Hill, who unflinchingly allowed me uncommon latitude in writing the book as I thought it should be written.

G.J.

IN

THE

BEGINNING...

I am all that has been and is and shall be,
And no mortal has ever lifted my veil.

— INSCRIBED ON THE LONG-GONE TEMPLE OF THE
   NATURE-GODDESS ISIS AT SAIS, EGYPT

Pretend for a moment that you are millions of years back in time past. For just a little while pretend that you are one of the first prehumans on earth, one of the most distant ancestors of what will—some three million years later—be known as *man*, the lord and ruler and "highest form of life" on this planet. In your prehistoric form, however, it would be presumptuous and preposterous to call you "human." Hominid (prehuman) or humanlike is the most complimentary term one could use. As looks go, you are not even as "handsome" as the hulking, hairy Neanderthal man of the Stone Age. He will be your descendant, but even his Stone Age is more than two million years in the future.

You are one of the weakest and most defenseless creatures on this earth. You have no powerful jaws, no venom or sting, no sharp fangs or razor claws; you do not have even a tough protective hide. You have no language to communicate with your fellow hominids, beyond some coarse grunts signaling "food" and "danger" (the two things that dominate your life) and a few other basics.

You have no skills. You have yet to discover that a tree limb can be a club, that a rock can be a missile, that fire can be a defense—and you wouldn't know how to light a fire, anyway. You are still a food-gatherer and scavenger. You have learned neither to hunt nor to make traps. You live on berries, nuts, grubs, weaker creatures you can run down and catch—lizards, insects and such—and sometimes on the rotting leftovers from the kills of fiercer animals.

Your only tool and only weapon is your brain, but that is still a poor and undeveloped organ. You utilize your scant intelligence mainly to seek a hiding place out of danger. Still, your IQ is already some degrees higher than that of the other animals. You can at least consider the world around you and dimly puzzle over what things are and why, and what they mean, which is more than the other animals can do.

This rudimentary power of reasoning doesn't give you much

comfort. Quite the contrary. It makes you feel surrounded by bewilderment, terror and hazard. The other creatures, operating by mere instinct, seem to accept their world unquestioningly. You, with your smidgen of brain, have begun to think about your world—if what you do can be called "thinking"—and all you can perceive is chaos, confusion and calamity, most of it seemingly out to get you. You see your fellow hominids killed by bigger or better equipped animals. You are menaced by inanimate things as well: falling tree branches, avalanches, quicksands. Even the weather is against you, with blizzards, floods, lightning, drought. And then, if nothing else is threatening you, you see your elders and others of your kind die from no apparent cause at all.

There is no discernible pattern to the world, no appearance of order, no way for you to understand its vagaries. Snow falls and the bitter cold comes. The snow melts and the weather becomes kinder, only to turn to storms or searing heat. Your memory span is too short for you to remember from one year to the next, to know that these are "seasons" and that they recur in regular succession. There is only one pattern which impresses itself on your dim, short-memoried brain: the constant and regular alternation of day and night. The day is light, no matter how bad the weather. You can at least *see* to indulge in your two prime occupations: foraging for food and dodging other beasts eager to feed on you. But then comes night and all the hazards of darkness. True, there is moonlight, though that is inconstant. Also, your night vision is better than any of your descendants will enjoy. But even your eyes are not nearly so keen as those of such predators as the sabertooth tiger, which hunt by night.

Your world is perilous at best, in brightest daylight. By night it is unthinkably horrible. Your distant, most intelligent and sophisticated latter-day descendants will still endure lingering traces of your being afraid of the dark. For you, night is the time when the scariest beasts prowl, when the world rustles and rumbles and whispers with noises that you cannot put a shape to. It is the time when you—poor, thinking, fearful creature—huddle and tremble in your bush nest or cave or treetop and try to sleep your way safely through the black hours until . . . until *It* comes again and brings the blessed day. Of course you have no word for *It* or for day or for blessed. But you do know that when day comes you are not quite so helpless. You can see to feed, and you can see to flee, and you can live at least until the coming of the next night.

Other natural changes in your world are too slow moving for your meager brain to register them. But day and night alternate quickly enough for you to take notice and expect them. Night will come—you know it and dread it—but so will day, and your spirit brightens as does the dawn. That beautiful, warming, shining globe of *It* lifts above the horizon every morning and, even when shrouded in cloud, banishes the paralyzing darkness. You could not live without *It*. You yearn for *Its* appearance; in a later time this will be called a kind of praying. Perhaps you give a gladsome whoop of welcome when *It* comes; in a later time the whoops will be psalms and hymns of thanksgiving.

To repeat: you have no word for anything so magnificent as *It*, or even for your humble, dependent, adoring feeling for *It*. But your *It* will eventually be called by your descendants "the sun." And *Its* taking care of you, *Its* relation to you, *Its* meaning for you will eventually be called by many different words—one of which will be *God*.

Now come back from that time 3,000,000 years ago into the present, but not yet to be you again. For the next little while, pretend that you are a modern-day scientist engaged in an experiment and you are studying the print-out answer to a problem you have programmed into your computer. The print-out is a jumble of complicated equations written in abstract mathematical symbols. But you know that these symbols—and, indeed, all the stages of your whole experiment—are based on, and in accord with, certain fixed natural laws.

Those laws, unchanging, unchangeable, are obeyed by everything from the smallest bits of matter and minute surges of force to the most massive entities and energies throughout the curve of the universe. At the small end of the scale is the atom, the tiniest unit of an element—hydrogen, oxygen, carbon, or any of the 100-odd other elements. But the atom itself is composed of still smaller components—a nucleus of protons and neutrons around which whirl electrons like planets orbiting a sun. And there are even smaller entities acting in or upon the atom, of which we know very little. Scientists have given them names such as "positrons" and "psi particles," though even their existence has yet to be positively proved.

As a scientist, however, you know that the atom is the basic building block of all matter and the source of all energy. Two atoms of the element hydrogen link together with one atom of the element oxygen and we have a single molecule of H_2O, or water. Atoms of various other elements link together in varying combinations to give us molecules of other, more complex substances, and those molecules combine into still other combinations to make the ingredients of everything that exists.

Now put aside your papers and walk to your laboratory window. Outside there are lawns and flowers and trees, birds and butterflies flitting about, people strolling on the paths. Everything you see—from grass blade to that distinguished looking gentleman who is the director of your research department—is composed of those infinitesimal, invisible atoms described in the computer-math symbols on your papers. You yourself may know the exact recipe for every ingredient of everything you see from your window. But if you were asked *what* put those atoms and molecules together just so, and *what* gave them life to make them move and act and live, you could no more answer the question than could that prehuman a couple of pages back and millions of years ago.

You raise your eyes from the laboratory grounds to the sky. In the blue are puffball clouds ("aerially suspended droplets of H_2O" to scientists). At dusk, you will begin to see the moon, the stars, the planets. You know that you are living on just one planet orbiting with eight others around the sun, very like those electrons whirling about the nucleus of an atom. And you know that your sun is just a single star in what we call the *Milky Way galaxy*. You know that this galaxy contains about 135 billion other stars—some or many of them undoubtedly the suns of other planetary systems. And you know that, farther beyond, there are perhaps another hundred billion galaxies of as many stars apiece. There are countless planets in all those galaxies, and it is almost a certainty that some of them harbor a form or forms of life.

With time enough, and radio telescopes strong enough, and computers competent enough, you could be the first scientist to calculate exactly how many galaxies, stars, planets, moons and other objects there are in the universe—perhaps down to the exact number of humans and other beings. You would find it all moving, acting, interacting in accord with basic natural laws. You would find that even the most immense galaxy of stars and planets and satellites is functioning with the precision and orderliness of the infinitesimal hydrogen atom's components. But never will you be able to tell—any more than could that prehistoric prehuman—just *what* laid out all this in the first place. What was *It* that contrived atoms, and of these atoms built everything from mud to men to moons? What was *It* that set all this machinery moving—electrons whirling about their atomic nuclei, planets orbiting about their suns, galaxies making their stately progress around the curvature of the universe? And what *keeps* all of this moving and functioning so orderly, precisely and everlastingly?

As in giving a name to the positron, which cannot even be proved to exist, men have coined many names for that unknowable something which created the universe and made so-called natural laws and oversees everything. That something has been called "Spontaneous Origin," "Mother Nature," "Creative Evolution," and the "Action of Chance." Another term for *It* would be "God."

SUN, MOON

AND

EARTH

SPIRITS

*On a hill at Bomma near the mouth of the Congo dwells
Namvulu Vumu, King of the Rain and Storm.*

— SIR JAMES FRAZER

There once lived a people so long ago that we have no record of
what they called themselves; thus some historians have given
them the contrived name of Indo-Europeans. Their original
homeland was in what is now Austria, Czechoslovakia and Hun-
gary, but through the centuries they gradually dispersed west-
ward across Europe and eastward as far as India. Their language
gradually evolved, in the different places where they settled, into
the languages spoken today in almost every country of the western world. Linguists have been able to work backward, so to
speak, from our modern languages and thus discover a number of
the original Indo-European root words from which many of our
words are derived. One of their words was *gheu*, pronounced
"gay-oo" and meaning "to invoke"—that is, to pray to or call upon
some Higher Power for a favor or boon.

Over the eons, as the Indo-European language evolved and
fragmented into our modern tongues, *gheu* underwent various

changes in pronunciation and one considerable change in meaning. It became *deus* in ancient Rome, *theos* in Greece, *dieu* in France, *bog* in Russia, *god* in the English-speaking countries.

Most people assume that *god* and *good* must have come from the same source; it would seem only natural. (The English long ago compressed the expression "God be with ye" into "goodbye.") In fact, *good* did come from the Indo-European mother tongue but from a different root word entirely: *ghedh*, meaning "fitting, proper." It may strike you as strange, but the English word *god* is more closely related to *giddy*, which nowadays means either "dizzy" or "silly," but earlier (in Old English) meant "possessed"—that is, "in the grip of some supernatural spirit." In olden days, madmen were believed to be not ill but inhabited by some god or devil.

In the previous chapter, I used the word *man* to signify all of humankind. Most writers do, when they need such an all-encompassing word. But to refer too often to *man* in that sense tends to give the impression that human beings everywhere developed at more or less the same pace and in much the same ways. This is obviously not true.

However, many books, which trace some aspect of civilization from the dawn of the world to the present day, speak of man as if he were a single, individual, eternally living "one man." In these books, man progresses from the cradle to crawling, to his first fumbling steps, to the awkwardness of adolescence, to the excesses of youth, to the high intellect, morality and skills of maturity. (Whether such a book was written in the sixteenth century or yesterday, the man of the time is usually considered to have arrived at maturity.)

Actually, man had different beginnings in different parts of the world and in different environments—forest, jungle or desert. He had fair weather or foul, a soft life or a hard one, to contend with. He did not just grow up simultaneously and identically everywhere in the world. Babies in a nursery may look alike when newborn, but you and I know that they will grow up to lead very different lives. Some may not grow up at all. Just so, the clans and tribes, even widespread cultures and whole civilizations in diverse parts of the world, took diverse pathways of development, and at

different tempos. Some of the paths were dead ends, and those civilizations no longer exist. Some of the paths ended in stagnation; today American and Russian space ships soar over primitive jungle tribes still living in the Stone Age. Some of the paths led to the numerous highly civilized but vastly different cultures we see in the world today. And one of the most important factors in shaping, invigorating, stalling or destroying this multitude of different life-styles was the God or gods the people chose to worship.

It is almost an indisputable certainty that the sun was the first god of prehumans all over this planet. To the hominids of long ago who were just beginning to evolve from beast instincts toward a dimly reasoning intelligence, the sun was the giver of warmth and light, the banisher of dread darkness. As those prehistoric creatures evolved still further over the course of countless ages, they learned that when the sun was high and hot in spring and summer the world leafed-out to produce edible fruits and vegetables. It also brought out of their winter dens such greenery-eating animals as deer and rabbits, which man could easily kill.

These early men learned, as well, that the sun would dry their meat for storage against a time when game might be scarce, and that this same sun would help cure the hides of animals to be worn as clothes (not for modesty, but for protection against the sting of cold and thorns).

Man would be around for another immeasurable span of ages before he ever conceived the notion of "god." Nevertheless, by all of today's standards and definitions of a god, the sun *was* the god of our earliest manlike ancestors, even if they didn't know it. Their general inclination was to regard the sun as a living being, like living beings on earth, but foremost of all living beings. The sun was the *life-giver*. In spring and summer it rose earlier, shone more warmly and stayed longer in the sky. Therefore it had to be the most full-of-life thing there was.

These are all surmises, but they are quite logical ones, and are reason enough to say flatly that "the sun was the first god of all mankind." However, we do have circumstantial evidence in the many artifacts (manmade objects) still remaining from ancient times, as well as the few peoples who have remained primitive and in the Stone Age right up to the present day.

You surely have heard of the circle of huge upright rock slabs called Stonehenge, on the Salisbury Plain in England. These stones were already ancient when the Britons were savages wearing bearskins and painting themselves blue for ornamentation. Whatever earlier and more advanced culture set up that circle of standing rocks, the people were demonstrably sun worshippers. Only comparatively recently has it been noticed that certain spaces between the slabs are precisely placed to admit the first rays of the rising sun on the longest and shortest days of the year. Stonehenge was most likely a crude temple dedicated to the sun, with sun-worshipping ceremonies held on those longest and shortest days.

As for modern-day primitive tribes, the Red Karens of Burma, until the turn of this century, wore the tattoo of a rising sun on their backs. The Igorots of the Philippines wore a sunburst tattoo on the back of one hand.

Those prehistoric hominids, as we have seen, naturally preferred the sun's brightness to the night's darkness—and, as a natural corollary, light and the color white would be regarded as "good," darkness and the color black "bad." The Plains Indians of North America would not kill a white (albino) buffalo. In Thailand to this day an albino elephant is held sacred; only the king may own one, and he bedecks the beast with precious draperies and priceless jewels. In the jungles of Central America, the Indians—supposedly now civilized, supposedly devout Roman Catholics—still won't fell a ceiba tree. Its trunk and limbs are ghost-white, its leaves a ghostly pale green. On a rubber plantation there, I was shown one ceiba known locally as the Godmother Tree. If an Indian plantation worker has some minor problem, he'll go and discuss it with the nearest Roman Catholic priest. But if he has some really weighty trouble, he goes instead to the Godmother Tree, prays for help or guidance, and slaughters a chicken or a piglet as a sacrifice to be left at its massive roots. Don't smile at these seemingly simpleminded attitudes. You and I and millions of other people believe in or are still affected by the age-old preference for white and aversion to black.

A bride wears white at her wedding to symbolize her purity, but also as a "good omen" for the new life she is beginning. At funerals we wear black; Death has stalked among us. Many people unforgivably still believe the light-skinned races are superior to the darker ones. They rationalize this in all sorts of ways: the whites were the first and best civilized; the darker races are still several rungs below on the ladder of evolution, and so on. But the white supremacists, in their heart of hearts—though few have the intellect to realize it, and fewer still would admit it—are (like the most fearful prehistoric hominid) in the superstitious grip of that primal yearning for the light and horror of the dark.

Sun worship—and the supposed superiority of light over darkness, white over black—has inspired foolishness, too. Otherwise intelligent people, who still believe in ghosts, almost never claim to have seen one by daylight; ghosts, they assure you in all solemnity, walk only by night. Even those people who don't believe in such things refer to midnight as "the witching hour." And in the more simplistic Western movies and TV horse operas the good guys are the ones with the white hats and white horses, the bad guys dress in black and ride black mounts.

But let's get back to prehistoric times. As you might expect, the pure-white moon was revered, too, though not so much as the almighty sun. At its full, the moon defeated *some* of the terrors of the night. But even then its light was markedly less than the sun's, and soon dwindled, and the moon gave no warmth at all. It was obviously, like the sun, a living being—its waxing and waning must have seemed the pulsations of slow breathing—but it was also obviously inferior to the sun. So some primitive peoples regarded the moon as the sun's little brother or, more often, the sun's wife.

Very well, if the moon was the wife, and patently the weaker of the two, then the moon was female and the sun male. Ever since those prehistoric times, down through the historical epochs that teemed with gods, the deities associated with the sun—Ra and Amon of Egypt, Helios and Apollo of Greece, among many others—have been mostly male gods. Those deities associated with the moon—Selene and Diana of the Greeks, Luna of the Romans, among others—were mostly female goddesses. To this day, many English-speakers refer to the sun as "he" and the moon as "she." It is the same in every other language with which I am familiar, where nouns are divided into masculine and feminine genders. *El sol* and *la luna* in Spanish, for example. As I have said, though, there were exceptions: there were cultures in which the moon was regarded as a sort of little brother to the sun, and therefore the male deity associated with the moon was a rather minor god, as in ancient Babylonia, where the moon god was known as Sinn.

As prehistoric man's intellect, curiosity, ingenuity and courage continued to develop, however, these qualities developed along different lines in the various clans and tribes. For some millions of years, man had been a scavenger and a hunter. But then some primitive genius invented either the fishhook (probably a sharp, bent bone) or the net (probably of twisted vine tendrils)—we will never know which came first—and another genius hollowed out the first boat from a tree trunk. Finally, some prehistoric hero, instead of fishing from the shore, dared to put out to sea.

Eventually there were tribes whose main occupation was

fishing, and over the years they began to perceive a connection between the phases of the moon and the size of their catch. (Fishermen today depend on scientifically calculated "solunar [sun-moon] tables" to determine the best times for good fishing.) The men of the Stone Age, of course, never recognized that the moon had anything to do with the sea tides, but they did know it had *something* to do with the success of their fishing. So, although they still didn't think in terms of gods or goddesses, these fisherfolk came to consider the moon (whether as "he" or "she") as their chief life-giver, and relegated the sun to second place.

Then other prehistoric peoples discovered that they could tame certain animals, breed them, and raise herds instead of having to chase wild game all over the forest. These groups became shepherds, cattle ranchers, goatherds. To them also, the moon assumed a new importance. For, like the women of the tribe, on whose childbearing the tribe depended for new members—and like the cows, ewes and nanny goats on which the tribe depended for sustenance—the new moon, slender as a maiden, every month swelled like a woman with child until it was as globular as that woman on the verge of giving birth.

We can surmise that the men of such tribes wished their wives and animals would imitate that dependable and frequent "pregnancy" of the moon, and present them with hordes of children to help with the work, hordes of calves, lambs and kids to increase their herds. Though such tribes were still eons away from thinking in terms of deities, they naturally regarded the moon as female, and set her above the sun as the prime life-giver.

The shepherds, cattlemen and goatherds had to do a good deal of moving about, forever seeking new pasturage for their herds. But along came yet another primeval genius who discovered that plants could also be "tamed," their seeds collected and planted in one convenient plot of ground. This was the beginning of farming—and the beginning of civilization because now whole tribes settled in one place to stay and cultivate their crops. No longer having to spend their time chasing about after wild game or wandering herds, they now had leisure to invent things and develop new talents. Besides learning to grow grain, vegetables and fruits for themselves, they grew fodder to support enough cows, pigs and fowl to provide them with meat, milk, eggs and hides. They learned to grow cotton and flax, and to spin thread and weave cloth.

The farmer folk now had to depend on a totally different life-force from the skies: the rain. The sun and the moon were dependable, but the rain was capricious. It might decide not to fall, in which case the crop withered, the farm animals died, and the whole tribe could face death from famine. Or the rain (generally regarded as a male "being") might decide to be too abundant, in which case floods would wreak havoc. So the farming tribes came to consider the rain as *their* Number One life-giver. They were forever wishing—this would later lead to ridiculous "magic" invocations and *much* later to prayer—that the rain-being would come when, and only when, they wanted him.

You will note that all these life-forces—sun, moon and rain— were believed to send their blessings from somewhere inconceivably high above the earth. That is why, when men did get around to believing in gods and goddesses and human souls and an after-life, the abode of the gods was always located somewhere high in the sky (or at least atop a high mountain), and the Heaven to which the souls of good people went after death was also assumed to be situated there. And when, at the same time, men began to believe in anti-gods: devils and demons—and a Hell for the bad souls—it was only natural (what could be more horrible?) to locate all of them in the perpetual darkness under the earth.

In regarding the sun, moon and rain as living beings, with feelings and wills of their own, and in giving them separate sexes, the primitive peoples were doing what is called *anthropomorphizing* them. That word is a tongue twister, but all it means is "seeing human qualities in nonhuman things." For example, Walt Disney anthropomorphized everything from mice to teapots. In terms of human character, Mr. Sun was considered a he-man, staunch and steadfast. Miss Moon (or Mrs. Sun) was willfully inconstant, but at least consistent in her moods. Mr. Rain was fickle and undependable, but welcome when he visited at the right time and didn't overstay his welcome.

Once a man had imbued these entities with humanlike qualities, it was inevitable that he should come to consider them closely akin to his own human self. He probably talked to them, whether aloud or silently, imploring or wheedling them to continue their bounties. This was another step along the way to prayer; though, as we shall see, there were to be numerous detours along the road to real religious worship.

Once the primitive man had anthropomorphized the sun, moon and rain, it was only a short jump to his ascribing "being" and humanlike personalities to other things in the world about him. The first would have been his chief source of food. Hunting tribes would identify with whatever game animals were most numerous in their vicinity. Herders would see human characteristics in their tame animals. Farmers would ascribe human quirks to their main crop—maize, rice, beans, or whatever—"generosity" when the plants produced abundantly, "stinginess" and "stubbornness" when the harvest was scant.

Next to be endowed with a humanlike "spirit" would have been the things that a particular group of people most admired or feared or were simply impressed by. Hunting tribes, for instance, might admire the superior hunting abilities of the wolf or bear. Fisherfolk might admire the fishing talents of the otter or the killer whale. (Here were the origins of the much later American Indians' adoption of various such admirable creatures as "totems"* for their several tribes and clans.)

A farmer might fear Mr. Rain's frequent companions, thunder and lightning, and anthropomorphize them into angry beings. A wandering herdsman might be impressed and awed by the unclimbable height of a jagged snow-capped mountain, and give it a humanlike "spirit"—almost certainly of the masculine gender.

Some people took a certain thing to have "being" and personality simply because it was so abundant. Many tribes living in heavily forested places in all parts of the world have considered the trees their kin and equals, if not their superiors. After all, the trees were there first, the tribesmen probably felt like intruders, and it was only prudent to be respectful to the forest giants.

A contributing reason for anthropomorphizing and eventu-

---

* Sociologists have adopted the word "totem"—from the Ojibway Indian language—to use for all such tribal spirits, though of course various other peoples had their own words.

ally worshipping the trees could have been that the people learned, especially when they began to plant orchards of their own, that some trees "mated" just as men and women did. Lest you find this hard to believe, let me remark that in my back garden I have two large fig trees: one wild coprifig which "fertilizes" the other, a cultivated fruiting fig. Were the coprifig to be cut down or die of disease, the other would cease to bear fruit. The primitive mind would have seen this as "mating" when the "husband" died, his "widow" would stop "childbearing" and "go into mourning."

It is not too difficult for us to understand how prehistoric man came to believe that living, or at least moving, things like trees and grain, sun and rain contained an animating, humanlike spirit, with mind and feelings. But, as I have mentioned, some tribes attributed these same characteristics to mountains, others to stones and similar inanimate objects. All right, a mountain is so majestic and dignified that maybe it just doesn't ever feel like prancing about and giving evidence of its human likeness. But a *stone?* A silent, unmoving, unimpressive lump? Well, if you looked at it through the eyes of a primitive, you would see even a stone as occasionally evincing human behavior, usually not the best behavior. As anthropologist Robert R. Marett once wrote, primitive man would decide that a stone has a mind and will of its own "if it behaves queerly—if it refuses to be chipped into a tool shape and cuts his finger instead, or emerges in the midst of the rapids and upsets his canoe. Nay, it need not act queerly; it is enough if it seems about to do so by looking queer."

We no longer believe that stones do naughty things deliberately, but even we modern folk can often see in a rock or cliff a "queer" resemblance to something else. We often give it the name of that something else, and frequently it becomes a showpiece for sightseers. An example is Profile Mountain in New Hampshire, whence The Great Stone Face looks impassively out over a lovely valley. That particular anthropomorphized lump of rock has been immortalized in one of Nathaniel Hawthorne's best stories. The Great Stone Face will live on—a prehistoric man would have said "live" and meant it—long after we all are dead and gone.

MORE

SPIRITS

AND THE

BIRTH OF

THE SOUL

*There is nothing in the mind
that was not first in the senses.*

— JOHN LOCKE

Rocks and mountains were "beings" that lived forever, insofar as prehistoric man could tell. The sun, moon, rain and other weather phenomena were eternally recurrent. The very trees seemed almost ageless; a man seldom saw one fall unless he chopped it down or lightning blasted it. Even the lesser animals seemed longer-lived than himself. Wild animals (and many tame ones), when they are ill, usually crawl away to some hiding place to die, so hunters almost never saw an animal dead except when they or some other predator had killed it. Herders and farmers generally butchered their beasts before they had a chance to die of disease or old age. When animals did die of a sudden, it was usually because of a drought or flood that could be blamed on the rain spirit. But man—and this goes for all men at that time—seemed, to himself, to live a life that was "poor, nasty, brutish and short," as the philosopher Thomas Hobbes would describe it many centuries later.

Prehistoric man had grown ever so much more intelligent, clever, creative and courageous. He now invented tools and weapons, discovered the many uses of fire, knew how to build a permanent shelter (house, hut, igloo or the like), knew how to defend himself and his family against dangerous beasts. Of course, he was still at the mercy of human enemies, and such natural hazards as avalanches and forest fires. But he also saw his fellow humans die of no apparent cause at all. The cause, of course, would have been some disease, but there was as yet no comprehension of such a thing as disease. Also, many a person died of simple old age. That, as anthropologists have concluded from study of prehistoric burial grounds, would have been at about the age of thirty. Every other living thing in the world seemed to have a stronger life-force and spirit than puny man. Though he was by now coping with his environment, man still felt almost as inferior to everything as he had when he was still a prehuman huddling and trembling in the dark.

This—early man's "inferiority complex"—was what made him move on, intellectually, from regarding everything in nature as having a humanlike spirit to regarding those spirits as superior to his own, and to do his best to rally the spirits "on his side." Now he began to sort the spirits into "good" and "bad" ones. The sun and moon were, of course, the best spirits of all to those tribes which held one or the other to be the prime life-giver. The rain was a sort of neutral spirit, since it might be either beneficent or malevolent at whim. Thunder, because it was frightening, and lightning, because it could be lethal, were bad spirits. The game animals, the herd animals, the corn, or whatever might be a people's mainstay of food, all bore good spirits.

The members of one's own tribe naturally had good spirits, except for murderers, thieves, woman-stealers and such, who were either killed, permanently maimed or cast out. If there was an unfriendly tribe living near by, or a marauding band that swept down and plundered more peaceable tribes, these obviously had bad spirits.

As you'd expect, not every people everywhere would agree on which entities were good or bad spirits. The fisher tribes would see a good spirit in all the waters of the world, while a landsman would dread anything bigger than a well or spring, and consider a white-water river or the fearsome sea as a being of most evil spirit. This whole book could be filled with a listing of the various nature spirits that our prehistoric ancestors believed in, because so many of them would have to be repeated under the categories of *Good, Bad* and *Neutral,* according to how they were regarded by different peoples in different places and in different circumstances.

The next step, clearly, was for man to devise ways to *keep* the good spirits good to him, and to ward off the harassment of the bad spirits. When a hunter killed an animal, he would caress its carcass, address it with respect, ask its forgiveness while he skinned and quartered it, thank it for presenting itself to be killed, and much more of the like. It was his hope, his belief, that the animal's spirit would go back and tell the other animals that it was a privilege to be slain by such a gentlemanly hunter.

This is not just mere conjecture, because many primitive tribes have practiced such ceremonies into historical times. The

Ainu of far northern Japan until quite recently held bears in high regard. The bear is in fact the most intelligent of all forest animals. It is psychologically quite close to man in its ways of responding to the world around it, and often walks on its hind legs. Furthermore, a skinned bear looks uncannily like a human being. So the Ainu believed bears to be real people who wore fur only for disguise when roaming in alien territory, and that when back home they shed their heavy overcoats, walked on their hind legs, and behaved like any other humans. So, when a hunting Ainu killed a bear, the entire tribe would engage in complicated and respectful ceremonies so that the bear's spirit would be certain to return home and assure the other bears that to let themselves be slain by the Ainu was an honor and opportunity they shouldn't miss.

Likewise, until recent times, when an Eskimo was out ice-fishing in a particularly good spot, he would carefully place all the fish he caught in a circle around the hole in the ice, with their heads pointing toward the hole, while he murmured thanks and extravagant compliments to the fish. It was his belief, too, that the fish spirits would pass the word to the other fish that he was a gentleman worthy of being hooked by.

Unlike hunters, fishers and herders, the farmer couldn't very well caress the being on which he mainly depended: the rain. Besides, there were times when he regarded it as a good spirit to be wooed, and times when it was a bad spirit to be fended off. So farming tribes developed various complex ceremonies to be used in time of drought to induce the rain to come, and in time of prolonged cloudburst to induce the rain to go away. You can still see Indian tribes in the desert of the American Southwest do their rain dances, though nowadays it would be hard to find an Indian who believes that a rain dance has any effect in bringing rain. He knows that it now brings free-spending tourists.

Ineffectual as such ceremonies have always been, they—like so many relics of early man's belief in nature spirits—have persisted into modern times. In a season of drought, the African Zulus used to bury their children up to the neck in the powdery, dry ground, then stand around the sweating youngsters and wail loudly at their plight. This was supposed to make the rain spirit (called Usondo) "melt with pity" at the sight—that is, to weep rain.

Even presumably devout, God-worshipping Christians of recent times have been known to resort to similarly foolish and futile methods of producing or preventing rain. The Roman Catholic French peasants, in time of drought, used to bring out of the church the statue of their village's patron saint and dunk it in the nearest pond to show the saint what they wanted: water. Italian peasants, also Roman Catholics, did the reverse. They would bring their patron saint's statue out of the church and stand it in the hot sun to show him or her what they were enduring.

Mexico, where I live, has a climate ranging from the subtropical (like Florida's) to tropical (like that along the Amazon), and most of the country has only two seasons: the wet and the dry. In the jungly, southernmost state of Chiapas, when the rainy season was late in arriving, I have seen the Chamula Indians—also nominally Roman Catholic—fetch the statues of several saints from the local church and suspend them from a tree limb head-down over a smoking smudge fire to make them feel even more keenly the heat and suffocation the Indians were suffering.

But, again, back to prehistory. Now we are talking about comparatively recent prehistory—perhaps ten thousand years ago. By that time most peoples were as intelligent as we are now, though of course far more ignorant than the least educated illiterate of today. Lacking any means of scientific investigation as to "how the world worked," they used their vivid imaginations, and came up with some concepts that seem pathetic, comical, weird, or even horrible to us moderns. But the concepts appeared to fit the facts and phenomena of the various primitive peoples' environments, so the people were satisfied for a good many more ages with their "explanations" of life and nature. The thunder was storm clouds bumping together. The lightning was a lance thrown by some sky-high invisible spirit. And so on.

By then, most human beings' brains had developed good memories, too. Unlike the dimwitted hominids of millions of years earlier, they could, for instance, realize that the seasons rolled around as regularly as day and night. Of course, the seasons vary in different parts of the world. In the tropics and subtropics, there is only a wet season and a dry season. In the polar regions, there are also two seasons: one of nearly 24-hour daylight and the other nearly 24-hour night. But let us confine our attention here to the temperate zones of the northern hemisphere, where most of the world's people live, and where there are four seasons: spring, summer, autumn and winter.

Seasonal changes were of minor concern to the hunting and fishing tribes. In cold weather, certain game animals, fish and birds would go into hibernation or migrate out of range, but winter was the time when other creatures were abundant—and in warm weather, the several species of game changed places. So there was always something to hunt or fish for.

To herding and farming peoples, however, the recurrent changes were vitally important. To the herder, spring was the time to take his beasts to pasture. By summer, when they had grazed all the lowland greenery, he would herd them to the uplands, even high into the mountains, where the grass would be new and fresh and abundant. Late autumn was the time for butchering, so that the winter's natural refrigeration would preserve the meat. (Sheep, like cattle and goats, were bred only for meat. It would be another 6,000 years before men learned to shear, spin and weave the wool.) And the coming of winter required the herder to find or build shelter for his animals and to feed them on hay and grains he had collected during the more clement months.

To the farmer, spring was the time for sowing, summer was the time of most abundant growth, autumn was the time for final harvest, and winter was the time for staying in his hut and living off the products of his labor. So, to both nomad herders and sedentary farmers the start of every new season was an occasion for festivals and ceremonies, asking the spirit of that season and all the associated spirits (sun, moon, rain, wind, and so on) to be especially good spirits this time around.

Even these early, unlearned and unscientific peoples had already taken note of the vernal equinox (about March 21) and the autumnal equinox (about September 22), the time when the sun crosses the equator and the length of day and night is almost precisely equal. That March date is the first day of spring, the September date is the first day of autumn. People also knew that June (again, around the 21st) brought the longest day in the year and the beginning of summer—though often called Midsummer's Day—and December 21st or thereabouts brought the shortest day, longest night, and the beginning of winter.

Naturally, great ceremonies were held at the time of the vernal equinox to celebrate the coming of spring, the time for planting and sowing. These rites involved not just individual tribes, but gatherings of tribes, sometimes from scores or hundreds of miles away. The celebrations included—besides invocations to the numerous spirits involved—feasting, frolicking, singing and dancing. Indeed, these rites in honor of nature spirits were the beginning of both music and dance as enduring parts of our cultural heritage. The works of Beethoven, the ballet, and the rock music of the Beatles—all are rooted in those prehistoric rituals. As we shall see in later pages, the belief in nature spirits ("animism," as anthropologists call it) also gave birth to art and architecture.

Horrible as it seems to us now, these springtime ceremonies very often included sacrifices of animals and not infrequently human beings, especially young maidens. Women, after all, were the lifebearers of mankind. Spilling their blood on the soon-to-be-sown farm fields—or so reasoned those believers in animism— ought to inspire the nature spirits to make the fields bear as fruitfully as women did.

The beginning of winter (also often called Midwinter's Day) was an equally important occasion. But it was not a time for frolic; it demanded solemnity and dignified dances and wailing chants of sadness. For the sun had been rising later each day, pale and cool, never very far above the horizon, and setting earlier—until one day (about December 21) became the shortest of all. Now, every human knew that this happened only once each year, and that the next day would be longer, and the next day longer still. But man had not yet (and never has) lost his horror of night. Who knew but that *this* might be the year that the sun would keep on going lower until it *never* rose again?

So these shortest-day ceremonies were even more important than those on the other ritual days. Great bonfires were lighted (they were also lighted on the longest day of the year), to remind the sun that human beings and the whole world needed heat and light. Many more sacrifices were made—again, often human sacrifices—because the spilled blood was warm as the summer sun, and red as the sun is at rising and setting, and because no human or other animal can live without blood . . . or without the sun.

Although these primitive peoples thought of their sometimes foolish, often hideous, and always useless ceremonies simply as ways of pleasing the good spirits and humoring the bad ones— they were actually practicing what today is called "worship." To quote Dr. Marett again: "Man was well on his way to religion before he thought about it at all."

Strange as it may seem, we have preserved a good many of those prehistoric practices. Indeed, practically all of us today, of whatever religion, still celebrate those heathen rituals to the seasons. The Christian Easter, Christmas, St. Patrick's Day have all been borrowed, directly or indirectly, from those old-time new-season celebrations. So have the Jewish Passover and Day of Atonement, the Muslim holiday called *l'ansara*, and numerous other holy days in other religions.

Those prehistoric peoples of the temperate zones, though they never invented a calendar, figured that each new year started—not in midwinter, as now—but with the vernal equinox, the first coming of spring and buds (which is really much more logical). Only comparatively recently did the Christian countries pick the First of January to start the year. As a matter of fact, your own great-great-great-great-great-grandfather may have celebrated New Year's Day at the same time of year his (and your) Stone Age ancestors did, because in Great Britain and the American colonies, New Year's Day still fell on March 25th until as recently as 1753.

There was one matter that greatly puzzled prehistoric man. He believed himself to contain some kind of animating spirit which enabled him to move, think, hunt wild animals, make love, fight off enemies, and so on. As a matter of course he endowed everything in nature with a similar spirit. But what exactly *was* that spirit? Most "thinkers" of the time located it (in man *and* beasts) in the head, where most of the sense organs are situated —sight, smell, taste and hearing.

But where did this spirit go when a person or an animal died? Perhaps, whatever it was, it got smashed or thrown out of the body when a man was brained with a stone axe or trampled by a mammoth. But what of those people who died quietly, of no apparent cause? A man looking at his dead friend could see no difference after death. There was nothing missing from the head or elsewhere about the body. The only difference was that the dead man no longer moved, spoke, worked, or fought. Maybe the dead still went on *thinking*; a person couldn't be sure about that. Or did the spirit perhaps leave the body behind, an empty husk, as a snake casts off its old, dried-out skin and moves in a bright and glossy new one? In which case, where did the dead man's spirit find *its* new abode?

Prehistoric man could not frame a definitive answer to any of those questions nor could he verify any of his speculations. Of course, neither can I. Neither can any modern-day philosopher, physician, preacher, mystic or theologian (a student of the nature of religious truths). The major religions of today assure us that the life force—or "soul," as we call it now—is undying, everlasting and either (*a*) leads some kind of life after death in Heaven or Hell, (*b*) persists as an invisible wraith wandering in this world, or (*c*) passes into some other earthly body, perhaps that of a totally different kind of creature, and goes on forever assuming a new body each time the old one dies.

These concepts are no more provable than were the puzzled primitive man's speculations. The various religions take their beliefs on faith, and demand no proofs. Anyway, science can offer no alternative to religion's assertion that the soul is God-given and that at death it returns to God for his decision as to what kind of afterlife it shall lead. As pointed out earlier, scientists today know every atom of the physical body of every sort of living thing, but the wisest of them still have no idea of what gives the living thing *life*. We may never know. It may have been intended that we should never know.

But prehistoric man was as imaginative as he was inquisitive. He was quite able and ready to make up an explanation for anything. If it seemed to fit the facts as he knew them, he would then take his own explanation as right and true. (Things bumping together made noise; therefore, thunder was caused by clouds bumping together.) In the case of the soul or life force or spirit, of course, he had no more facts to work with than we do today. So the explanations he concocted as to what the soul was and how it worked (there were widely varying theories among different peoples) were sometimes wild and farfetched. But the thinker of those long-ago times was ready to accept as *proved* anything that couldn't be *disproved*.

There is no knowing how many different theories prehistoric peoples came up with as to the nature of the soul. But archaeologists have dug into Neanderthal graves of some 50,000 to 75,000 years ago and found that the dead men of that long ago were buried with their flint tools, stone axes, and bits of food. It is obvious that his fellows figured a dead man would need his earthly goods in some kind of afterlife, though what Neanderthal man's idea of an afterlife may have been we cannot even guess. However, we do know something about the beliefs regarding the soul held by primitive tribes in historical times. For example, many peoples have believed that a man's soul is expelled in the last breath he exhales. This has led to some weird behavior on the part of his survivors.

On Pulau Nias, a volcanic island off the western shore of Sumatra, a dying chief's throne would be inherited by whoever could catch the chief's dying breath in his own mouth or in a bag. Since a chief had several wives, hence numerous sons, and since even nonrelated males could compete, any dying chief's last hours must have been made hideous by all the would-be chiefs clustering, elbowing and fighting around his pallet to catch his last gasp. It happens that the houses on that island are built on stilts as a protection against floods. It is told that one cunning chap became chief by lurking under the dying chief's house, boring a hole in the floor beside the old man's pallet, and inhaling the chief's last breath—and soul—through a long, hollow reed.

Some peoples have believed that nobody is really *born* with a soul, but must be ritually *invested* with one. In other words, that a newborn child is just a lump of living matter and requires a ceremony of "second birth" before it can truly be regarded as human, or even qualify to be given a name. This ceremony has varied from place to place, but—like so many other primitive rituals—we still have it with us in the Christian act of christening, when the baby is sprinkled with "sin-cleansing" water and then is given the name it will bear all its life.

Speaking of children, you may recall Operation Babylift, the 1975 evacuation of Vietnam which brought thousands of orphans to the United States from that war-ravaged land. Many American families adopted one or more of these waifs, and the new foster parents were coached in how to make the children feel at home in their foreign surroundings. Among the instructions: never pat the child on the head. This caress, however gentle, is not bestowed in Southeast Asia, because there the head is still supposed to be the habitation of the soul, and anything that touches the head might annoy or even injure the soul. The Javanese, until quite recently, would not even wear hats. The Cambodians used to build only one-story buildings, so that no one could live over the head of another.

Many tribes living along sea coasts used to believe (and still do, among ignorant peasants in such places as Brittany, Wales and Spain) that a dying man, no matter how near death he might be, or however agonizing his pain, could not die until the sea's tide began to ebb, thus drawing the man's soul out with it. A natural counterpart to this was the belief that a pregnant woman, no matter how hard she labored, could not give birth until the tide came flooding in, bringing the new baby's soul with it.

A variant of this belief—and one that is rather pleasant to contemplate—was held by the Haida Indians who lived on the Pacific Coast of North America. They believed that a man about to die would see a vision of a canoe, paddled by his old and dear friends who had "gone before," now coming in on the flood of the ocean tide and beckoning him to join them and depart for the Spirit Land when the tide turned and ebbed out again.

Almost all primitive peoples have believed that their names, their shadows, their reflections in a mirror or in still water were "fragments" of their souls. I can testify, from my own explorations among jungle tribes, that they know what photographs are, yet still regard a photo as capturing and carrying away some fraction of their life force. On one occasion, among the Tzeltal Indians of Chiapas, I had my camera torn apart—and was lucky not to get hacked apart myself.

To this day, Orthodox Jews will not give a new baby the same name as that of any living member of the family. Now it is only a respected tradition, but it originally stemmed from a fear of dwindling the life force of both parties by "halving" it between them. In ancient Germany, it was believed that a dead man's soul joined his living brother's soul, thereby adding to the brother's life force, courage, intelligence, life expectancy, and so on.

The notion that one's soul can be stolen, either piecemeal or entire, arises from the age-old belief that the soul can be separated from even a living body—and indeed often briefly departs on its own. That belief was inspired by men's dreams. In their long-ago dreams they (as we do in ours) sometimes found themselves in far-off places, either familiar or totally strange to them. Or they were visited in their dreams by other people, alien or familiar, and some of the latter had been long dead. Who could ask for better proof that the soul could go voyaging on its own— and that it still lived after the body's death?

Since it appeared that the soul did most of its gallivanting when the body was asleep, in almost every primitive tribe it was forbidden to wake any sleeping person, even if he was asleep on the job. His soul might be off on a jaunt somewhere, and if he awakened while it was absent, he was doomed either to die or to live out his life as a limp, unmoving, unthinking idiot.

Today you'll still hear the advice: never wake a sleepwalker; just keep him out of danger until he awakens on his own. The reason given sounds ever so medical and reasonable: a sudden awakening will mean a dangerous shock to his nervous system. This is simply not so—unless you happen to wake the sleepwalker when, say, he's standing on the edge of a roof. It is merely one more superstition left over from that ancient belief that he might awaken without his soul.

Since dreams about deceased friends and relatives "proved"

that the souls of the dead were still wandering about, some primitive peoples have made a try at building imitation human figures for them to inhabit and thus feel more or less alive again. In the land of Assam, some tribes set up life-size wooden manikins around their villages for dead souls to move into. However, woodboring wasps moved into them instead—leading the Assamites to believe that dead souls transmigrate into wasps, a belief to which they have ever since paid great respect. Most people pay a wary respect to wasps, anyway, but if one of these Assamite tribesmen is stung, he doesn't swat or even curse. He simply assumes that he's being reprimanded, perhaps by his late grandfather, for some sin or error he has committed.

It has long been believed that the soul, though invisible to the human eye, must have *some* materiality and therefore *some* weight, however minuscule—and that a body *must* become a tiny fraction lighter at the instant of death. In past centuries, ghoulish experimenters would lift a poor dying wretch onto a scale to measure the abrupt lightening of weight as he breathed his last. But no scale was delicate enough (or so they reasoned) to detect the difference. Nowadays, more scientific investigators still test dying persons by lurking around their deathbeds with infrared and laser cameras in hope of getting a snapshot of the soul departing in the form of an "essence" or "aura." To date, no one has succeeded.

Maurice Maeterlinck's 1910 fairytale-allegory *The Blue Bird* pictured Heaven as teeming with sweet little new souls eagerly waiting and yearning to be born as babies on earth—a pretty fancy. But twenty-two centuries earlier the great Greek philosopher Plato had asserted that there are only a fixed number of souls, that never has a new one been created, and that a dead person's soul simply is transmigrated, to appear in the next baby born. Well, in Plato's day, there were an estimated 75 million people in the whole world, presumably owning all the souls there were. Today, there are nearly 3.75 *billion* people in the world. If Plato was right, some 3,675,000,000 of us are walking around right now with no soul at all.

DETOUR

INTO

MAGIC

All magic is black, in that it clouds man's reason and stunts his growth toward wisdom. If we can learn anything from magic, it is simply that the only darkness to beware of is the darkness of the unenlightened mind.

— GARY JENNINGS

There is an old saying that is still current: *"Everybody wants to go to Heaven . . . but not just yet."* It is not as old, of course, as the prehistoric times we are discussing, but it could have applied very well to our early ancestors. Even after they had conceived the idea of their having immortal souls and some kind of life to look forward to after death, they still were not at all eager to die. Indeed, from the earliest hominid to the most devout churchgoer of today, very few persons in the long roll of mankind have ever wanted to die. For who can be sure as to what comes afterward? All of us hold tenaciously to the life we know, and try our best to make that life enjoyable and long.

One of the ways in which early man tried to improve and lengthen his life was by influencing the world and all its spirits to be good to him, by means of magic. This happened among different peoples in many places at widely varying intervals. Indeed, there is no known civilization, settlement, tribe or clan of early humankind that did not, in one way or another, go through a long period of depending on the foolish futilities of magic.

As we noted earlier, the Neanderthal hunters of 50,000 years ago evidently believed in an afterlife, hence they must have had some concept of a human soul. It may have been another 40,000 years before the more civilized farming tribes got the same idea—perhaps by noticing that the grass grew greener at an old grave and, from this, concluding that the buried man's life force had passed into the grass. Similarly, long stretches of time may have passed between one people's putting their trust in magic and the same sort of belief arising among another people in a different part of the world. Curiously enough, however, no matter how far apart those cultures were—in thousands of miles or eras of time—the magic they practiced had basic characteristics that were almost identical.

In the first place, primitive man invested almost everything in the world with a life spirit similar to his own. He knew that he was a creature of hungers, desires, moods, many fears and a few hopes, many weaknesses and a few strengths. It was easy enough, then, to believe that everything else in nature could be influenced in the same ways that he could. And so, when the river flooded to his very doorstep (its spirit hungry and grabby, it seemed) prehistoric man undoubtedly tried to pacify it and send it back to its normal course by tossing into it every scrap of food he could spare. When the sun went into one of its terrifying eclipses, and its life spirit seemed threatened, all men came to its aid by whooping and howling to scare away its "attacker" spirit, whoever he might be. Magic of this sort is called "ritual magic"—that is, ceremonies in which large groups, tribes or even whole nations would take part. Ritual magic was used to deal with the major problems and the more powerful spirits in early man's world, to call for favors from such good spirits as the sun, the seasons, the local game animals, etc., or to ask the good spirits' protection against such evils as the storm, the flood and the drought.

But meanwhile each man needed help in his individual day-to-day doings. He needed luck in his hunting, fishing, herding or farming. He had to have something to heal his wounds or cure his stomach cramps. He wanted some assurance that his children would be born strong and healthy. For solitary concerns like these, no matter how important they were to the individual, it was hardly practicable to have the whole tribe turn out for a ceremony to invoke ritual magic. None of the other, necessary tasks of life would ever have been attended to.

And so, gradually, over the centuries, the job of making magic was entrusted to one man in each tribe or community who, in turn, was relieved of all other responsibilities. Sometimes the post was given to the oldest and wisest member of the group. Sometimes it was an hereditary honor, handed down from father to son. Sometimes a man sought the post because he was lazy— and it was an easier job than hunting, farming, or fighting off enemies. Or perhaps he had been crippled in battle or in the hunt, and this was the only civic service he could perform. In any case, the man usually had more than average intellect and shrewdness. The magic-maker was seldom the actual chief of the tribe—the strongest man generally ruled—but even the strongest ruler would come to him for counsel before an important venture. The magic-maker soon became indispensable as man's go-between with the spirits. Despite the claim of many other still-practiced professions—that is, any occupation requiring training, hard practice and advanced study—*the first* and oldest profession is that of the magic-maker.

The magic-maker has been called by many different names in different places and times—names which have been translated as "medicine man," "witch doctor," "wizard," "sorcerer," "mage," and so on—but most sociologists lump them together under the name *shaman*, a Russian word describing the magic-makers of ancient Asia. In earliest times, the shaman's job was to make what is called "white magic"—that is, to communicate with the spirits via spells, incantations and ceremonies intended to do good for his people. He knew exactly the right way to smear a stone spear with eagle's blood to imbue it with the eagle's spirit so the spear would fly, like the eagle, far and true. He was the medicine man who could doctor a hunter's wound by calling for mercy from the spirit of the wild boar that had gored him. The shaman knew what words to say and what gestures to use when he planted a tree at the time a baby was born, so that the child would absorb

some of the tree's spirit and grow up, like the tree, sturdy and straight. Most of his magic was based on the widespread belief that every spirit in nature resembled every other spirit to some extent, and therefore must have a similarity of behavior. The shaman simply took this theory—"like produces like," or what today is called "imitative magic"—and applied it to whatever magicking he was required to undertake.

Suppose that for some reason the deer in the vicinity of a hunting tribe had suddenly become scarce. For a long time no deer had been seen, and the tribe was suffering from lack of meat and hides. The tribe's hunters knew from experience that if only one single deer showed up, they could be sure that the rest of the herd would soon follow. So, on the principle that "like produces like," the shaman would dress himself in a set of antlers and a deerskin and go prancing deerlike through the surrounding woods. He looked and acted like a deer; therefore, to the primitive mind, he *was* a deer; therefore, all the missing deer would soon return and join him in the hunting grounds.

Such imitative magic has persisted through the ages. Doctors of only two centuries ago would prescribe to patients with "brain trouble" that they eat a lot of walnuts, becaue the meat of a walnut looks rather like a tiny brain. Until the turn of this very century, bald men rubbed bear grease on their shiny pates, for no reason but that the bear has an abundant coat of hair.

The most favored bouquet for a bride at her wedding used to be a posy of orange blossoms. Not only did they prettify and perfume the ceremony but they also symbolized a leftover of imitative magic. Orange blossoms on the tree bring forth fruit (unlike, say, carnations or roses), therefore they should work similar magic in making the new bride a fruitful mother of many children. The confetti still thrown at newlyweds as they leave the church is symbolic of the same thing; the flakes of confetti are substitutes for seeds.

Old cowboys and prospectors I have met out West in the United States still won't wear any underwear but long red flannels. Long and flannel, okay, but why red? The wearers probably don't know it, but red flannel has long been supposed to be warmer than undyed flannel, because red is the color of fire, and fire gives heat.

Another primitive belief (that the soul can leave a man's body and go meandering on its own) caused the prehistoric shaman to become an expert in dispatching his soul on missions to negotiate with the spirits. To do this, he had to be able to put himself to sleep on short notice or at least pretend to do so. Some shamans did this by dancing until they fell unconscious from exhaustion. Some fasted until they fell into a coma from near starvation. Some made a fire of cedar twigs and inhaled the pungent smoke. Some ate ivy leaves, as intoxicating as liquor. When early man discovered how to make beer and wine, it was a great boon to the shaman; he could even more easily drink himself into a stupor.

If the shaman merely fell down and slept for a while, he would awake to report his dream dealings with the spirits. If he went into convulsions, it meant that he was actually wrestling with whatever spirit he had business with. Sometimes, unconscious or pretending to be, he would go through quite a performance. For example, since disease was still a mystery to early man, it was assumed that a man who fell ill had simply and temporarily lost his soul in some way. The shaman would go into his trance and send his own soul searching after the missing one. This journey might require that his soul climb mountains, swim rivers and even do battle with evil spirits—all of this would be acted out by the shaman's body back at the tribal camp, while the whole tribe looked on in awe and admiration. It was the only entertainment those people had—watching their shaman twitch and writhe and scamper about. So, in addition to song, music and dancing, we can add acting as one of our modern arts which are derived from those prehistoric tomfooleries.

Sometimes a shaman might genuinely be an epileptic—that is, a person afflicted by a brain malady who may at any time be seized with a convulsive fit. Anyone suffering from severe epilepsy can be thrown into convulsions by a sudden noise, a cold draft, a surge of emotion. Presumably, an epileptic shaman could be thrown into a fit merely by someone's suggesting that he commune with a spirit.

Many shamans had assistant, or apprentice, shamans to interpret to the tribe the gurgles, groans and shrieks they uttered while in the presence of the spirits. One nineteenth-century explorer has described how a shaman on a South Pacific island "became violently agitated, and worked himself up to the highest pitch of apparent frenzy, the muscles of his limbs seemed convulsed, the body swelled, the countenance became terrifying, the features distorted, and the eyes wild and strained. In this state he rolled on the earth, foaming at the mouth . . . and, in shrill cries, in violent and often indistinct sounds, revealed the will of the spirits. His attendants received and reported to the people the declarations which had thus been received."

Omitting the last several words, this could be a modern case report of any poor wretch wracked by a fit of epilepsy. The word *epilepsy* in fact comes to us from ancient Greece, where it meant "a seizure (by the spirits)." In many tribes, a child who showed a tendency to epilepsy delighted its parents. Instead of trying to cure its affliction—if there had been any cure available in those days, which there wasn't—they encouraged the unfortunate youngster to learn to *trigger* his attacks. In this way he was sure to grow up to be an important, respected, easy-living shaman.

Most early shamans were male, but in some places women had an "equal job opportunity" in that field. In ancient Germany, for example, it was believed that *only* women could communicate with the spirits. A woman could do this by staring for a long time into the swirling eddies of a stream until she was literally self-hypnotized. When brought out of her trance, she would then report on what she had learned from the spirits, or whether they had acceded to whatever tribal request she had transmitted.

Naturally, there were other primitives besides the shaman who were epileptics or suffered delirium from some illness, or just plain went crazy. These were assumed also to be possessed, but by an evil spirit, and it was the shaman's job to cast out that spirit. We have all seen pictures of African and American Indian witch doctors cavorting to perform this rite of driving the evil spirit out of the afflicted one.

The belief that a lunatic is a person "possessed" by a devil lingered on until less than two hundred years ago. The Roman Catholic Church still preserves among its numerous rites one for exorcising demons and devils from persons and dwellings which are believed to harbor such beings. Among intelligent priests, this holdover from prehistory is considered flagrant superstition, and it has become something of an embarrassment to the Church as a whole. It is very seldom practiced by any priest nowadays, except in the most backward parishes, and will probably soon be prohibited.

The rite goes like this. The priest, after making all sorts of signs and gesticulations, sprinkles holy water about and says a number of prayers. Then he puts his hand on the afflicted one's head and intones: "I exorcise thee, unclean spirit, in the name of Jesus Christ. Tremble, O Satan, thou enemy of the faith, thou foe of mankind, who hast brought death into the world, who hast deprived men of life, and hast rebelled against justice, thou seducer of mankind, thou root of evil, thou source of avarice, discord and envy . . ." and so on. The recitation is quite long, but this catalogue of insults is supposed to drive any but the most stubborn demon from the sufferer's body.

So far we have been discussing the prehistoric shaman's trade in white magic. But eventually the shaman found it even more profitable to deal in black magic—the kind that is intended to harm. An occasional person would ask him for a magical favor that could only be granted by hurting someone else. For instance, if a farmer coveted another's barley field or one herder wanted another's pastureland, the easiest way to get it was to arrange for the rightful owner to be driven away or killed. And the easiest way to do that was to bribe the shaman to exert his powers, perhaps promising him a share of the ill-gotten grain or a portion of the herd. Thus the shaman saw in black magic a way to gain more power, wealth, ease and honor for himself—by inflicting humiliation and misery on his trusting fellows.

So long as a tribal shaman dealt only in white magic, he was supposedly consulting the good spirits, asking favors of them or enlisting their protection against the bad ones. But when he came to practice black magic, he claimed to have friends among the evil spirits as well. Partly because of his own ambition to be high and mighty, and partly because he couldn't help fearing the evil spirits just a little himself, the shaman gradually set up rules for his people to follow to avoid risking the spirits' anger. Then he set himself up as the one to decide how the rules should be obeyed and to punish those who failed to observe the rules properly. Most of these rules undoubtedly were of the "thou shalt not" variety. Today they are commonly called *tabus*, a word borrowed from the South Pacific islanders which means "forbidden for supernatural reasons." In a prehistoric hunting tribe, a typical tabu might have been: "Thou shalt not eat the best piece of meat." Because it was reserved for a sacrifice, perhaps to honor the sun spirit, perhaps to curry favor with the storm spirit, but generally meaning that it wound up in the shaman's stomach. Every culture was hedged about by its own particular set of tabus, but they all boiled down to: "Thou shalt not do *anything* without the permission of the shaman!"

The manner of the shaman's climb to power has been strikingly similar in every society. It was always based on the fact that he dealt in things that simply did not exist (such as nature spirits), or things that he invented himself (or that his predecessor shamans had invented), or natural phenomena that he turned to his own purposes. Therefore the shaman could manipulate them —and wield a whip over his people—as he chose.

In at least one case, however, black magic evolved somewhat

differently. We have all heard hair-raising tales of the magic called voodoo, supposedly the practice of the blacks in Haiti, New Orleans, the Gullah islands off South Carolina, and numerous other places in the New World. It is believed to include the casting of death-dealing spells and the existence of zombies, the "walking dead." Actually, voodooism began as the quite innocent religion (or *vodu*) of the Mandingo and Ewe tribes of western Africa, who worshipped numerous nature spirits. (One of them was named *mamagyombo*, which we have made into mumbo jumbo, and now use the word to refer to any solemn but meaningless ritual or utterance.) The only striking thing about this religion was that a person cut his hair in a distinctive style to show which spirit he particularly favored.

But then the greedy chiefs of these tribes began to sell their subjects, first to Arab and then to western slave traders. As slaves in America, the Mandingos and Ewes were "converted to Christianity," but they continued to hold their *vodu* meetings whenever they got a chance, purely to remind them of their heritage and the old country. Though their *vodu* by now was nothing but a sort of mutual comfort and aid brotherhood—not unlike the Elks or Kiwanis fraternal societies of today—their secret meetings disturbed the other slaves and even their white owners. The Mandingos and Ewes were practicing black magic against them, or so the others believed.

Well, "give a dog a bad name . . ." as the saying goes. The slaves were the lowest class of people in America. So some of the shrewder blacks, to enhance their own status, set themselves up as *hungans* (shamans) of black magic. A *hungan* terrorized his fellow slaves with dire threats—he would send a "walking dead" zombie to strangle anyone who crossed him—unless the other blacks paid reverence and blackmail. These self-appointed shamans were feared and catered to and "bought off" by blacks and even by many whites. Although voodoo is as nonsensical as any other black magic, it is still believed in by the more ignorant blacks and whites in the Southern United States and throughout the West Indies.

We have already discussed imitative magic, which was mainly used for beneficent white magic. When the shaman branched out into black magic, he invented a system which today we call "contagious magic." *Contagious* means "by contact," and this form of magic assumes that things which have once been in contact with each other will continue to have some effect upon each other. It is best illustrated by the widespread belief that one can physically injure an enemy by doing harm to a doll image of him. Into this clay or wax doll is kneaded some hair from the enemy's head or lint from his clothes, or the like. Stick pins in the image or hold it over a fire, and the enemy, wherever he may be, will feel the pain.

This belief in the vulnerable image has been common to cultures as far apart in time and space as ancient Babylonia, Egypt, Greece and Rome, the Indians of North and South America, and all of Europe in the Dark Ages. It is still believed in and practiced to this day among the more primitive tribes of Australia, Africa and Malaya, not to mention the ridiculous "witch cults" and "devil-worship religions" which keep springing up even in civilized societies.

The fear of contagious magic has been so long-enduring that many people still insist on burning their nail parings, hair clippings, and so on, to prevent their falling into an enemy's clutches. This precaution has been especially true of chiefs, kings and other rulers, because they have perpetually feared their underlings' ambitions to assassinate them and usurp their thrones. Among the Betsileo tribe of Malagasy, for instance, there used to be specially selected men called *ramanga* whose only job was to follow the chief around, to *eat* his fingernail and toenail parings, his hair clippings and, if the chief accidentally cut himself, to lap up the spilled blood.

A sort of combined black-and-white, imitative-and-contagious magic was practiced by the aborigines of Australia. When one of these primitive people got a toothache, he would have his tribe's shaman enchant the pain into a black stone. (Many shamans were adept at hypnosis long before the modern world heard of it, and doubtless could dull many pains merely by telling the hypnotized patient that the pain had gone away.) The black stone was thereafter called a *karriitch*, and was kept by its owner until the advent of a war with another tribe. When battle was joined, the warriors would throw their *karriitch* stones at their opponents in order to give *them* the toothache and thereby hamper their fighting ability.

Since it is apparent that the shaman held his honored position in every tribe only through his people's childish belief in his efficacy and his own make-believe, and since real magic or actual communion with nature spirits is impossible, you may wonder how he could make his magic even seem to work. Well, in the first place he had to be a clever man to have attained his high office, and if he didn't remain exceedingly clever, he lost it. In the second place, the mere laws of chance would assure that a shaman's magic or predictions would succeed once in a while. And such is human nature (now as then) that one occasional "hit" impressed his people more than any number of "misses." But the shaman also knew how to stack the odds in his favor. He would make a public pronouncement that could be interpreted in two or more ways, thus improving the chance that the promise or prophecy would fit whatever actually happened. When his magic charm or a prediction failed, the shaman would usually defend himself by attacking someone or something else. If he "made a pact with the rain spirit" but got no rain, he might announce that another shaman somewhere was casting counter-spells. In which case, all rainmaking attempts would have to be postponed while he went through a string of enchantments to cancel out the other shaman's interference. If he labored at this task long enough, you see, eventually the weather conditions *would* be right for rain-making.

In all fairness, it should be said that not every shaman was a fake and a fraud, deliberately deluding his fellows. Many shamans were sincere in believing that they had exceptional powers and *really* did have some influence with the spirits. Such men would keenly feel the responsibilities of this distinction. A shaman who honestly tried to use his powers to good purpose could only be dismayed when those powers failed to work. But, on the other hand, a sincere shaman would seldom hold his job for very long. Believing in his own enchantments and spirit contacts, he would be ill prepared to explain why they so often went wrong. The only really successful shaman would have been the politician-type who, if he could not often supply a desired magical effect, could at least always provide a glib excuse.

And, although magic—with its multitude of shamans, wizards, witches and the rest—has persisted even to this day, in most places only the politician-type magic-makers have survived. The sincere shamans have had a harder and harder time of it. Modern medicine gradually has become available even in the most remote communities. The sophisticated white man invaded dense jungles and isolated islands, bringing "true" religions, banishing "pagan" beliefs, and pooh-poohing or punishing those savages who insisted on maintaining their heathen ways.

In the Pacific group of islands called Papua, less than a hundred years ago a shaman named Tata Ko complained piteously to the English governor: "If a man falls sick, his family come to me and ask me to make him well. If I don't do something for him they say, 'Tata Ko, the medicine man, desires that our brother die,' and they are angry and perhaps will try to kill me. If I do give them some help, they insist on paying me for it, and you arrest me on a charge of blackmail by sorcery."

In Mexico, the shamans are still believed in by the backwoods Indians, and are divided into two classes: *curanderos* (medicine men practicing white magic) and *brujos* (witches practicing black magic). The *brujos* are much feared while the *curanderos* are much respected.

(I trust you will understand why I frequently refer in this book to the customs of my adopted country of Mexico. It is because I prefer, whenever possible, to cite happenings I have seen with my own eyes, rather than regale you only with things I have learned from the experiences and writings of others.)

Not long ago, and again in the jungles of Mexico's southernmost state of Chiapas, I was privileged to watch a Zinacanteco *curandero* at work. He was an aged, ragged gentleman named Antún, which is the name of the Zinacantecos' rain spirit. Antún spoke no Spanish and of course no English; he knew only his native dialect. But I had brought along a Spanish-speaking Zinacanteco to interpret. Antún told me, through the interpreter, that to date he had cured 208 people of various illnesses. "But," he confided, "it is not really I who do the healing; it is the great spirits. Whether people come complaining of their heart, lungs, or whatever, it is mostly a sickness of the soul, of the vital force— and that is in the keeping of the mighty spirits."

On this day, Antún was to cure a mild stomach upset in his own wife. He began the ceremony by burning incense and chanting before a flower-banked wooden cross in the dooryard. (The cross was a sacred symbol in many American Indian cultures long before Columbus crossed the ocean and brought the Christian cross.) Meanwhile, two of the *curandero's* daughters had dashed off to catch one of the family chickens. The ceremony moved inside the adobe house, where the ailing woman lay on a floor pallet. Candles were lighted around her, and the old man, still chanting, passed the squawking rooster several times over her body (enchanting the ailment into the fowl). Then the girls tied the bird by its feet to a roof beam, Antún slit its throat and caught the spouting blood in a saucer. He daubed some of the blood on his wife's forehead, then bade her drink the rest of it. She did so, and said she was beginning to feel better already. However, I was less impressed by the *curandero's* magic than by the progress of civilization into this remote jungle. While her husband had been occupied with the outdoor part of the ritual, I had looked in on the ailing wife—and found her downing two aspirin tablets and a mug of fizzing Alka-Seltzer.

As I have said repeatedly, magic has persisted through the centuries from prehistoric times—medieval witchcraft, alchemy, "scientists" as misguided as the fictional Dr. Frankenstein, belief in monsters, ghosts and "the little people," down to the many superstitions that are still believed in today, and which are evident even in businesslike and orderly transactions. For example, when a man signs a check or a contract, it is considered fully binding on him, this being a direct descendant of the ancient belief that a man's name is a fragment of his soul. His failure to pay on the check or to deliver whatever he promised in the contract will endanger his own soul.

Now, let us follow primitive magic as it gradually finds a different direction, away from uselessness and witlessness, and toward beliefs that will eventually come to fruition in the concepts of gods and God.

FROM

MAGIC

TO

WORSHIP

Heartily know,
When half-gods go,
The gods arrive.

— RALPH WALDO EMERSON

Almost beyond a doubt, the first "god" that man ever recognized was a goddess. Among the earliest drawings and carvings made by prehistoric men that have yet been found are depictions of what archaeologists (with tongue in cheek) call the "Stone Age Venus." Such rude statuettes certainly do not remind one of the Romans' Venus, goddess of love and beauty. These 50,000-year-old figurines are of grossly fat, heavy-breasted, bulging-bellied females—each of them obviously the image of a woman very near to giving birth.

The male hunter or fisher of that time would have stood in awe of women in general, of some kind of Goddess of All Females, and perhaps even of his own mate. For it was only women who gave birth, thus ensuring the survival of the tribe—and no one knew how they did it. The men could not grasp the fact that their mating with a wife had anything to do with babies being born. As far as they could tell, the wife simply gave birth spontaneously or whenever she felt like it.

Some peoples—their development stalled at a Stone Age level—never *did* learn "the facts of life" until modern times. One Nigerian tribe, which regarded the moon as the prime life-giving spirit because it swelled like a pregnant woman, used to believe that the Moon Mother sent a Moon Bird flying down to earth to bring babies to the women. That myth is strikingly similar to our "baby-bringing stork" tale (which originated in Germany).

Of course, even back in the Stone Age, it couldn't have been too long before the more advanced peoples figured out the relationship between a man's mating with a woman and her giving birth nine months later. When it became obvious that women couldn't have babies without the cooperation of a man, the Mother Goddess was toppled from her pedestal. Man began to strut, and woman was demoted to the inferior position she held until quite recently in human history. In many later religions, however, whose mob of gods included a fertility deity in charge of making crops, herds and children abundant, the fertility deity was always a female.

The "Stone Age Venus," of course, dates from long before most peoples had even invented magic as a way of controlling and improving their lives. While the men who drew and carved those figurines doubtless considered women objects of mystery and wonder, there is no evidence that they actually worshipped them or indulged in any formal ceremonies of praise or prayer to them. So calling the Stone Age Woman a "Mother Goddess" is rather stretching the point. Anyway, that belief couldn't have lasted for very long, and most likely the believers, as in practically every other early culture, turned to believing in a multitude of nature spirits, then went through a long period of trying the influence of magic, before they approached anything like a concept of gods and devised a religion for worship.

Magic, as man's means of communication with the nature spirits, has had a long life. In most cultures, however, it gradually gave way to a crude form of religion. Of course, some people were to go on trusting in magic for ages, even into the present age. But people with good sense, even in prehistoric times, eventually came to realize that magic wasn't doing much in the way of swaying the major spirits that governed the most important as-

pects of their lives. They began to notice that the shaman, in demanding favors from nature, failed far more often than he succeeded.

They continued to believe that everything in their universe contained a spirit. But various peoples, one after another, decided that they had been wrong in supposing that all the spirits were more or less humanlike and could be influenced in the same way a man could. They came to believe that at least some spirits were of a nature far different from and more powerful than their own, aloof and unreachable by appealing to their "humanity." To these highest and haughtiest spirits, people began to say, "Please, I'd be grateful if . . ." instead of, "Look here, I want . . . !" as the shamans had done.

Such peoples were still a long way from practicing religion as we know it, but they had reached a crucial turning point. No longer would they *insist* on favors from the spirits, and hold ritual-magic ceremonies which rather resembled our "protest demonstrations" of today. Henceforth, men would *beg* for favors from the spirits. Their formal ceremonies would no longer be arrogant, but humble and meek. And when and if their supplications were granted, there would be (for the first time in history) further ceremonies to say a grateful "thank you."

That was, and is, the basic difference between magic and religion. A man no longer shook his fist at the spirits and demanded. He bowed his head or dropped to his knees and pleaded. He acknowledged that there were powers greater than himself, and abased himself before them. He knew that such powers could not be controlled. He could only hope that they might be flattered and coaxed into lending an occasional helping hand. And to help in making his cajoling more effective, prehistoric man began to seek a better mediator than the shaman had been. The replacement go-betweens that most cultures first selected to mediate between gods and men were mere humans, like the shamans—or at least they had been, for they were now stone-cold dead. It was the souls of their dead ancestors that those primitive people asked to act as messengers between men and the mightier spirits.

For a long time, men had held varying and opposing attitudes toward their dead. For example, most settled farming tribes, knowing that their sustenance came from the earth, assumed that somehow they had, too. (As did Adam in the Jewish-Christian story of creation.) When a person died, his soul went winging off to some afterlife and his body, being only an empty shell, was consigned once more to the earth, where its elements lived again by fertilizing the crops into greater abundance.

In contrast, the nomad tribes—hunters and herders—held a dread of the dead, both body and soul. They refused to pollute the earth on which their tame or game animals grazed. So they did not bury their dead, but burned the bodies instead, or left them exposed on platforms or in treetops, where scavenging animals, vultures and ants would soon dispose of them and scatter their bones far and wide. A body thus fragmented, figured the nomads, could hardly have its soul entire to haunt and pester them.

The Imerina tribe of Madagascar still repeat a myth that their long-ago ancestors came from a homeland far to the east of Madagascar in search of a "land where no one ever dies." (Evidently they did come from Malaya, for the Imerina grow yams, bananas and other crops which originated in Southeast Asia.)

After an intolerably long voyage, the tribal boats had landed on the coast of Africa. The black natives were hospitable; the newcomers never heard them speak of the dead, and saw no burial grounds anywhere; so they thought they had actually found the land where there is no death. Then they learned, to their horror, that these people *ate* their dead. The Imerina immediately set sail again, found the offshore island of Madagascar and, with life and death going on as before, gave up their dream of immortality. They still live (and die) on Madagascar.

Some people were happy to believe that the souls of the dead survived, and welcomed them when they appeared in the dreams of the living. These people were sure that the dead returned only to give timely advice or warnings on how to avoid trouble ahead. Other folks were not so glad to see the dead in their dreams. Why, they wondered, did the dead persist in hanging around the living? Were they angry at not being alive themselves? Were they envious of the living, and perhaps wished to do them harm? (Here was the beginning of the belief in malicious and terrifying ghosts.)

Many tribes buried their dead with their feet tightly bound or with thorns stuck into them, so they might not walk again—or with their hands tied, so they might not do mischief even if they did walk. Others chopped the head (the soul-container) off a corpse and buried it separately at a distance from the body. If the dead man did wake, he'd have no body to carry him around.

Some peoples—the Chinese, for one—had dual feelings of love and fear toward the souls of the dead. Those who had died by violence or accident, cut down in the prime of life—well, naturally they would be bitter about not having lived out their days. And they could be dangerous, for such a soul would haunt the place of its death until it could lure another victim to a similar end. This substitute would then release the haunting soul so that it could proceed on to the peace of the Afterworld. So, if a Chinese came upon a chap thrashing in a deep pond or a quicksand and calling for help, he would give no help. Obviously, the drowning man was being sucked under by a spirit who had died there sometime previously and was now arranging a substitute drowning. To rescue the chosen victim would be to anger the dead soul, and that wouldn't do. The rescuer himself might be the next victim.

However, the Chinese (and other peoples in places far apart) believed that a person who lived to a ripe old age and died peaceably had no reason for resentment or revenge. These would be the souls of fathers, grandfathers, great-grandfathers. The people who entertained this belief had always paid high respect to their elders when they were alive, and revered them even more when they were dead. So they quite naturally believed that these sage souls would be eager to do what they could to help their living descendants. They would bring dream-warnings of coming disasters, advice on when to plant and harvest, what girl a young descendant should marry, and so on.

Even better, since the souls could travel as easily as wisps of smoke throughout the spirit world, when a man had a favor to ask of the spirits, he would assign some ancestor's soul to relay it for him. The man himself might feel rather unworthy to address the spirits directly, but his wise and dignified old great-great-grandfather stood a much better chance of being listened to by the powers on high.

People who held such beliefs, though they continued to assume that there were higher powers directing their lives—from Heaven, the Spirit World, or wherever—gradually came to believe that those powers were so very high and mighty that mere man could not hope to communicate with them directly. Only the dead souls could do that, so the people focused their reverence and prayers on the ancestors, instead, and left it to them to handle negotiations with the higher powers.

The result was ancestor worship—the first organized form of religion. It was also the beginning of the priesthood—though as yet the "priests" were merely disembodied souls. In times to come, the priests would be mortal men and women ordained to conduct formal religious services, to help other men and women communicate with their gods, and to lay down laws of behavior for living a good life on earth that would lead to an even better life in the next world.

After ancestor worship came the worship of gods, though this came slowly and in various guises. Through much of man's early history, as we have seen, he believed that every animal, every stalk of grain, every tree had a separate life spirit of its own, resident within. Gradually men came to believe that this was not the case—that, although each man had an individual animating soul, other things did not. Instead, each species of animal, each kind of vegetable, and so on, had a single, all-embracing spirit—living, no doubt, somewhere up in the limitless skies—who looked down and directed the life and doings of the deer, the mullet, the barley, the vine, or whatever he was the spirit of.

The more a man came to believe in this concept, the more power he attributed to each of those spirits. The spirits now took on all the qualities of gods, as we would describe a god today. Since man had learned that they could not be controlled, and only rarely could be persuaded to behave generously, man did not see his early gods as beings of warmth and benignity. Instead, he saw them as surly, irritable, inimical beings who were easily provoked to rage and not easily cajoled into kindness.

In short, the early gods were not loving fathers but wrathful tyrants, and religion began with human beings worshipping the gods out of apprehension rather than adoration. Man's praise and sacrifices and thank-offerings were actually hypocritical, since all of these were aimed at trying to appease the gods' vanity, wrath, jealousy and ill temper. Not many years ago, an Eskimo told anthropologist Ralph Linton how his people regarded the god-beings: "We do not believe, we fear."

In a very few societies, where the people lived in warm climates with abundant game or fish and lushly growing fruits and vegetables—where life was easy and pleasant—so were their gods easy-going and warmhearted. Elsewhere, man's religions, the forerunners of our own, had their beginnings not in reverence of the gods, but in abject fright, anxiety and toadyism. It is still said that most people lead proper lives not so much in hope of Heaven as in fear of Hell.

Many societies believed that their gods were angry and unfriendly because they had been offended by some long-ago ancestors of the people. Before that offense, whatever it was, the gods had been kindly and good, and the people had lived long, long lives in joy and luxury. The Jewish and Christian religions still teach that the first man and woman lived thus, until they disobeyed God and ate the forbidden fruit. Eve and Adam were driven from the Garden of Eden, disease and death were introduced into the world, and men and women have had to slave and suffer ever after, in atonement for that "original sin."

Among primitive peoples, it was a common belief that if they could only make peace with the gods once more, they could return to that earlier, presumably happier life. They tried for a "peace treaty" in many ways. Some societies continued to sacrifice their most valuable animals, their captured enemies, even their own sons and daughters, in the hope that the gods would accept these offerings as making good for whatever the original offense had been. Others decided that if they could only cleanse every member of the community of his or her *present* sins, once and for all, they'd be given the chance to "start all over again" in a new Golden Age. This belief led to some strange ceremonies—"banishing the scapegoat," for one.

The best known version of this ritual is that of the ancient Israelites, who used an actual goat. With many incantations and prayers, a priest of the tribe would "load" the goat with all the sins of the people. Then the poor beast would be driven off into the barren desert, there to die of starvation, and the sins would presumably "die" with it.

Other peoples have loaded their sins onto a human criminal, a citizen picked by lot, onto chickens, pigs, llamas, apes, even boats in seaside communities. These would then be either killed or driven off to die of hunger or exposure (or sunk, in the case of the boats). The Chinese used to bury a jar filled with bits of crockery—each of which had been invested with one person's sins. The jar also contained gunpowder and a fuse sticking up above the ground. The fuse would be lit, the jar would explode and "destroy" all those sins.

The village of Onitsha in Nigeria was very businesslike about ridding itself of sin. At a specified time each year—and these years were not too long ago—any tribesman who had erred in some terrible way was allowed to make amends merely by contributing 28 *ngugas* (about ten dollars) to a sort of community fund. With the money collected, the village bought from some other tribe two of its sickliest and most useless citizens. These were brought to Onitsha, roped, then dragged along the rocky ground, by everyone who could get a hand on the rope, to the Niger River, while the accompanying crowd chanted "Wickedness! Wickedness!" all the way. If the wretches survived this treatment, they—and the sins of Onitsha with them—were unceremoniously drowned in the Niger.

We still say of someone who has misbehaved: "The devil got into him." In Cambodia, this was quite literally believed—that is, a man who sinned had been impelled to do it by an evil spirit. So, every March, each city in Cambodia performed a ceremony to expel those spirits and the sins they had caused. The city's citizens and countryfolk from miles around would gather within the city walls. Also herded into the city were all the elephants available.

On the night of the first full moon, volleys of muskets were fired to stampede the elephants through the city streets toward the main gate. This irresistible charge supposedly carried all the spirits and their sins before it (though the elephants probably did more damage than any number of evil spirits). When all the elephants had gone, a specially blessed rope of grass, painted in colored stripes, was strung around the city walls to prevent the spirits and their sinfulness from returning.

You will have perceived that these scapegoat and banishment ceremonies were nothing but leftovers of magic that had got incorporated into religion. And lest you think that only primitive religions were infested with superstition, let me mention that a Methodist church in Atlanta, Georgia, observes a certain ritual at every New Year's service. The members write down on bits of paper "the sins they would most like removed," and ceremoniously burn the papers in a pot beside the pulpit. Orthodox Jews still toss such bits of paper into running water.

There was one primitive society, however, that was unique in not forever looking back to a Golden Age. In fact it did not even revere its ancestors. Instead, the people of Polynesia looked forward. They had their deities—Tangaloa, god of the sea; Rongo, god of vegetation, and so on—and they held ceremonies in the gods' honor. But the Polynesian rituals were not like those of so many other cultures—wheedlings for a better life or a new start in some Garden of Eden. These islanders already lived in a paradise on earth. They hoped to better it by bettering themselves— to eliminate intertribal warfare, murder, theft and other sins—but they reckoned to do it on their own and without truckling to the capricious gods. Each Polynesian tribesman saw his tribe as "an upward-growing, outward-stretching tree." Each new generation was supposedly superior to the generation before, and in time the tribe would attain to perfection in all things. This could have made life complicated for the Polynesians, since, according to their beliefs, the eldest child in a family outranked not only its younger brothers and sisters but its parents as well (they being of the previous generation). Hence many sisters were "superior" to their brothers, wives "superior" to their husbands, and so on. Instead of confusion, however, this actually made for a degree of equality between the sexes that was unknown in any other society in the world. Elsewhere, women were automatically assigned to an inferior position. Each sex, of course, had its own duties, responsibilities and interests, but the Polynesians—thanks to their unique religion—were the first people ever to attain equal rights for men and women. Then came the white man with his religion . . . but that is another and sadder story.

As the gods proliferated in early times, their worshippers (or fearful subjects) classified them by grades, from most powerful to least powerful, but of course all were more powerful than man. In the majority of societies, the sun god was supreme. Everybody knew what he looked like: a round, bright thing, sometimes with rays emanating from his circumference. Second to the sun god, among hunting tribes, was generally either the god of the game they liked best to eat (say the deer) or the hunting animal whose prowess they most admired (say the wolf). The people presumed that the gods of those animals looked like those animals. Each tribe would adopt this particular animal as its totem, and would pay it reverence, and often would carve and paint elaborate totem poles bearing the animal's image. (To repeat: art is one of our cultural heritages derived from primitive beliefs.)

To illustrate how the religion of totemism generally worked, let us regard the aborigines of Australia. They believed that they were descended from a Dream Time when the *alchuringa*—a sort of combined man and animal—wandered the world, dropping little heaps of souls here and there. The souls had their choice of becoming men or animals. Thus, down to historical times, each tribe of aborigines had as its totem that animal which they believed had risen from the same heap of souls as had the tribe.

The aborigines of the kangaroo totem, therefore, would no more kill and eat a kangaroo than they'd eat one of their own fellows. But they had very cleverly figured a way out of their dilemma. The kangaroo tribesmen would dress up as kangaroos and chant and dance to implore the kangaroo god to increase the kangaroo herds. By mutual agreement, a neighboring tribe of the emu totem would beseech an abundance of flocks of that bird. If the ceremonies worked, then the kangaroo people could kill and eat their fill of emus, while the emu people would be amply supplied with kangaroo meat.

For other societies, visualizing their gods wasn't so easy. What did the god of corn look like? or, for that matter, the god of rain, of love, of music? Well, lacking any other point of reference, most peoples decided that these faraway and unseeable gods looked just like . . . people. The Old Testament assures both Jews and Christians that their God created man in his own image. "And," one cynical wit has remarked, "man has returned the compliment."

Both Jews and Christians refer to God as "He"—a male—and have tended to think of him as a majestic, dignified, grandfatherly figure. In Michelangelo's painting in the Sistine Chapel at Rome, God wears a flowing, silvery beard, but has a superbly virile and youthfully muscular body. You can all but feel the power surging from God's forefinger as he reaches out to awaken his creation, Adam.

The Greek philosopher Xenophanes wrote, 2,500 years ago, that African gods were black with flat noses, while the gods of the northern lands were blond and blue-eyed. He therefore speculated that "if horses had hands, horses would draw the forms of gods like horses." French philosopher Montesquieu expressed the same thought, 250 years ago, in saying that "if triangles had a god he would have three sides."

It was essential for the early believers to envision the physical aspects of their particular gods, for they soon began setting up carved wooden or stone idols to show the gods that they were honored, and to give the worshippers something visible and tangible to which they could pray and make offerings. Of course, a man could raise his face skyward and say a few words to one god or another whenever he felt like it, but people came to believe that by focusing their words of compliment, praise, petition or thanks on one point—the idol of whichever god could best help them—their prayers would carry more weight and have more effect.

In time, many peoples felt that worship itself would be more efficacious if they had someone to lead them in prayer—much as an orchestra works better with a conductor. And so one man would direct their services and ceremonies. He might have been the tribe's one-time shaman, or a descendant of a shaman, or simply a powerful-lunged, well-spoken orator. In any case, he was the forerunner of the priest, minister, rabbi, muezzin, bonze —all the reverend clergymen of the religions in the world today.

One after another, different societies also decided that their praying would be more effective if it could be done in a place apart from outside distractions. The idols that had formerly been set just anywhere about a village were now sheltered inside special buildings—sometimes one building for all the tribe's gods, sometimes a separate edifice for each. Now the worshippers could assemble and pray without being interrupted by wandering pigs and poultry, or by children at play.

Here was the beginning of true architecture. A man's own home might be thrown together in any old way and built of straws, sticks, clay, or whatever other material came ready to hand. But a god's house naturally had to be well constructed of the most handsome and durable materials to be found in the vicinity or imported from afar. It had to be designed as beautifully as that tribe's level of taste and notion of beauty permitted.

Almost all the primitive gods have been long forgotten, almost all the primitive religions long abandoned. But we have seen the crude beginnings of everything that comprises the living religions of today—the gods, man's belief in them, the idea of an afterlife, the acts of worship and prayer, sacrifices and thank-offerings, hymns and dances, the earliest "priests," the making of idols and of temples. All these would eventually be refined, simplified or elaborated, mistaken notions corrected, new gods substituted for old. But long before history had begun to be written, all the elements of modern religion had been put into practice.

A
GALAXY
OF
GODS

O Lord, my transgressions are many, great are my sins. Full of pain, I am overpowered, and dare not look up. To my merciful god I turn, proclaiming my sorrow.

— BABYLONIAN PRAYER OF 5,000 YEARS AGO

The ancient Egyptians had at least 2,000 different gods which we know by name. The Aztecs of Mexico had 45 major gods and some 1,220 minor ones. The average length of a chapter in this book is approximately 3,800 words. Therefore, if I stopped at the end of this paragraph and merely listed those 3,265 Egyptian and Aztec gods by name, I would fill this entire chapter. But that wouldn't tell you anything about those gods, and would mean ignoring the countless thousands of other gods recognized by other civilizations. Obviously, it will be necessary for me to pick and choose among this galaxy of gods in order to give you some idea of how different peoples in various places visualized their sometimes similar, sometimes unique, deities, and the many ways in which they chose to worship them.

In previous chapters, though we have occasionally encountered more modern gods, we have dealt mainly with those prehistoric ones which we know only by inference and educated guess

—from the artifacts (burial-ground contents, cave paintings, fragments of idols) and the persisting legends left by those peoples who had no written language. But now let us leave prehistory and skip to the time some 5,500 years ago when man first learned to write.

By that time, all but the most primitive societies had developed the full regalia of religion as we know it today—temples, priests, formal rituals of worship, holy-day festivals, the idea of some kind of Heaven for good souls and a Hell for the wicked. But no society had as yet attained to the concept of worshipping one single all-powerful Lord God. All these groups still had several gods, some had many, some had multitudes of them. However, such societies did rank these gods and goddesses according to the powers the people believed they wielded. So, in most cultures, there were two outstanding deities; generally one was male, the other female. The male was most often identified with "father sun" and the female with "mother earth." From the union of the two were supposed to have been "born" all animals, vegetation, human beings, and so on.

By this time, too, mankind was not a scattering of widely separated tribes, communities and cities. Trade had begun to be carried on between even widely dispersed peoples by land and by sea. Those groups which had developed in isolation were now exposed to contact with many other groups of different colors, customs, politics and religious beliefs. Many times, one society would so admire some god or goddess of another society that they would adopt him or her into their own religion. Let's look at two examples:

Babylonia, one of the first great civilizations of the Middle East (situated about where Iraq is today) in its early days worshipped a moon god named Sinn, and this Sinn had a daughter, Ishtar by name. Ishtar was first identified with "the morning and the evening star"—that is, the planet we today call Venus. But the Babylonians evidently found Ishtar much more glamorous than her father, and she gradually replaced him to become the moon goddess. Her popularity was such that her worship spread throughout the ancient world. Though Babylonia fell into decay and disappeared from the map, Ishtar went marching on. In Canaan, she was known as Ashtarte, in Phoenicia as Astarte, in Moaz as Athtar, in Ethiopia as Astar, in Egypt as Isis, in Syria as Atargatis, in Greece as Aphrodite, and finally in the Roman Empire (by which time Babylonia had been gone for 300 years) as Venus. By whatever name, however, she was always and everywhere regarded as the goddess of love and beauty.

The Persian god Mithras had a similar widespread and long-lasting popularity. In the weak last days of Babylonia, the Persians invaded from the north, took over that land and imposed on it their own religion, comprising many gods. Among these gods Mithras was only a minor warrior godling, but—what with the Persians being a warlike people—he was particularly revered. His worship soon spread as far as Assyria in the west and to India in the east, where he was known as Mitra (his name did not undergo so many changes as did Ishtar's).

When the Romans began their conquest of the then known world, as they extended their empire into the Middle East, they too encountered and adopted Mithras. A warrior himself, Mithras was an especial favorite of the Roman legions, but his cult flourished back home in civilian Rome as well. There were striking similarities between the Mithraic religion and Christianity, which was also just then coming into flower in Rome. We shall see later how such similar (or borrowed) beliefs caused clashes among the various competing religions, and changed Christianity (which, in its early days, was rather haphazard and easy-going) into an organized, formalized religion.

Doubtless much of that old-time borrowing of gods and goddesses was influenced by the greatest mass migration of any people at any time in history. These people were those arbitrarily-named "Indo-Europeans" mentioned in Chapter 2, who originated in Middle Europe. As they spread outward from there, various groups settled down in one or another of the lands they encountered. They must have been a forceful people, for, wherever they wandered, they planted their own language. That tongue has, over the ages, changed considerably in the different areas where they settled. But almost all the languages of the western world today—from English to Swedish to French to Russian, plus the Hindi and Bengali tongues of India—are ultimately descended from that migrant horde's "mother tongue."

Along with the language, they also brought their own gods, collected other deities from foreign lands they passed through, and "sowed" them again along the way, implanting them in the religion of whatever country they settled in. The Indo-Europeans' own chief god was the sun, Dyaus Pitar ("Father of the Sky"), and very shortly you'll see how he *almost* changed the course of history.

The oldest formalized religion of which we have any accurate knowledge was that of the ancient Egyptians, thanks to the many hieroglyphics (picture writings) that survive from as long ago as 3200 B.C. During Egypt's early history, the four ruling gods were Ra, the sun god; Osiris, the god of grain, greenery and growth in general; his wife Isis, goddess of love and beauty; and their son Horus, who presided over the underworld court which decreed the fate of dead souls.

When a man died, he descended to the underworld, where his heart was weighed in the balance against a feather in the opposite pan. If the court decided that the dead man was evil (of small heart, one presumes), he was immediately fed to The Devourer, a creature which was part crocodile, part lion, and part hippopotamus. If the deceased was deemed worthy of immortality, Horus led him by the hand into the glorious Heaven of Osiris.

Then, in 2050 B.C., a pharaoh from the city of Thebes ascended the throne and installed the formerly insignificant city-god of Thebes, Amon ("the hidden one") as the foremost of all the nation's gods. Ra, Osiris, Isis and Horus were demoted to minor deities. Amon was a demanding god, and his priests practically blackmailed the common folk into paying tribute, until the priests became so wealthy and powerful that they threatened the rulership of the pharaoh himself.

So the pharaoh Amenhotep III ("he in whom Amon is content") who came to the throne about 1411 B.C., did an unheard-of thing. Probably to augment his power by forming an alliance abroad and perhaps partly to spite the Amon priests, he took as his second wife a foreigner—Gilukhipa—a princess of the Mitanni, who ruled a nation in the area that is now southern Turkey.

The Mitanni were descendants of those far-wandering Indo-Europeans, and Gilukhipa brought the concept of Dyaus Pitar with her to Egypt, for her own private worship. But this sun god emerged from Queen Gilukhipa's boudoir and took on new stature after the death of Amenhotep III, when his and his first wife's son became pharaoh in his turn.

He took the throne as Amenhotep IV, but soon changed his name to Ikhnaton, "the effective spirit of Aton"—Aton being his translation of Dyaus Pitar's name into the Egyptian language. Ikhnaton's whole story is told in a companion volume to this book.* It is enough to say here that Ikhnaton—mostly out of his own convictions, but perhaps partly to honor his stepmother and her god—abolished the horde of Egyptian deities, including the mighty Amon, and decreed that henceforth Egypt would worship only the one all-powerful, all-knowing, all-loving Lord God, represented by "the radiant disk" Aton. Ikhnaton made Egypt the first civilization in the world to worship a single deity and Creator —even more extraordinary, the world's first *loving*, not just powerful, god.

The mass of Egypt's people—long impoverished and repressed by the demands of Amon, the 1,999 other gods, and their greedy priests—embraced this revolutionary idea. Unfortunately, defeats in war, a weakening of the Egyptian empire, and conspiracies among the out-of-work Amon priests toppled Ikhnaton from his throne. The next several succeeding pharaohs abolished Aton, restored Amon to the role of chief god, and all the other gods to their former places. But for this, the whole course of human history might have been different—and better—because Greece later borrowed many of its religious beliefs from Egypt, and Greece greatly influenced our present-day Western civilization.

The Greeks were contemptuous of all "lesser" cultures. (About 450 B.C., their great historian Herodotus sneered at the Egyptians as an inferior race. For example, he wrote, they had the barbarous habit of going to the toilet *indoors*, instead of relieving themselves in the street as the civilized Greeks did.)

* *March of the Heroes* (Association Press, 1975).

Contempt did not, however, stop the Greeks from appropriating whatever they found useful in other peoples' culture—especially other peoples' gods. For one, the Greek goddess of love and beauty, Aphrodite, was modeled on Isis of the Egyptians.

Even earlier, the Greeks and then the Romans had appropriated the sun god Dyaus Pitar, as that wave of Indo-Europeans passed through their respective countries. The Greeks changed his name slightly, to Zeus Pater; so did the Romans, to Jupiter; but both names still meant "Father of the Sky," and he became the foremost god of both Greece and Rome.

The Greeks borrowed their god of the seasons from the Assyrians, but bungled this a bit. In Assyria, and later in Greece, it was believed that this handsome young god was beloved by both the goddess of fertility and the goddess of the underworld, so the chief god (Ea in Assyria, Zeus in Greece) adjudged that he should spend half of each year alternately with each goddess. Thus he became the god of autumn and winter (when he went underground) and of spring and summer (when he rejoined the fertility goddess). In Assyria, this god was called Tammuz, but the people referred to him respectfully as *adon* ("lord"). The Greeks mistook the title for his name; hence in Greece he became Adonis.

The Romans originally had only a few gods of their own. They revered the two mortal men of legend, Romulus and Remus, who were believed to have founded the city of Rome. And, being a warlike and wary people, the Romans had a god of boundary lines, named Terminus. But the Romans were avid collectors of other peoples' gods. They inherited from the Etruscans, who had inhabited the Italian peninsula before the Romans came, two groups of gods called *lares* and *penates*. These were invisible little spirits, almost pets, which dwelt in the homes of deserving families and, like the brownies of fairy tales, helped about the house and brought good luck to all under its roof. Incredibly, in a sense they still exist. In legal contracts these days, when a homeowner sells or bequeaths his property to another, there will often be included a clause specifying that the house is handed over "with all its lares and penates," now meaning all its furnishings, decorations and valuables.

Practically every city in the world in those days (meaning "the known world": *i.e.*, the lands around the Mediterranean Sea) had its special, individual god. But in many cities the citizens never knew who their local god was. The city fathers kept that knowledge a close secret, and for a good reason. As the Roman Empire expanded and gobbled up one area after another, the Romans made a practice of sending spies into a city before they attacked it; the spies' duty being to learn the name of the city's protecting god.

Then, when the Roman legions besieged the city, they could make offerings and shout prayers to that city's deity, inviting him to desert the city and join the Roman side, where he would be highly revered, be given sacrifices (no doubt the citizens of the city, once it was captured), and then be taken back to Rome and given an honored place among the other Roman gods. It was for fear that their god might defect to the Romans—and thus leave their city without any supernatural defense—that caused city officials throughout the Mediterranean world not to trust even their fellow citizens to know the god's name.

Though the Romans plundered gods as well as booty, the greater number of their deities were adopted from those of Greece, sometimes complete with their Greek name, sometimes with a new one—thus Aphrodite became Venus in Rome; Persephone, the Greek goddess of the underworld, became the Romans' Proserpina, and so on—but always with the same functions. So we might as well consider the gods of Greece and Rome simultaneously, since they were practically identical, and so were the Greek and Roman modes of worshipping them—or, rather, of trying to stay on good terms with them. For, just as their prehistoric ancestors had seen every nature spirit as "humanlike," so did the Greeks and Romans visualize their numerous gods as being humanlike, but to a much greater degree.

These gods were believed to be able to assume any guise they chose—from absolute invisibility to the forms of animals, birds, storms, "showers of gold dust," and, frequently, human beings. In the latter shape, these gods and goddesses even mated with mortals, and their children were demigods—for example, Herakles (known as Hercules in Rome), who was born of the union between mighty Zeus and a mortal girl named Alcmene. Such offspring led "superman" lives as earthly heroes, thus winning their right to dwell with the other gods on Mount Olympus, the high cloud-shrouded peak in Greece, or (in Rome) among the clouds and stars of the heavens. The gods of both Greece and Rome exhibited human character traits to an exaggerated degree —including those which are far from admirable—regardless of what shape they happened to be wearing. Like humans, the gods were capable of love and hate, charity and revenge. They were jealous, fickle, lustful, hot-tempered, easily angered, stubborn, unpredictable, mischievous, helpful or hindering to man as it pleased their whim. The people built temples to them—the Greeks even built altars and shrines to "the unknown gods," lest they overlook any and thus insult them. The people paid a sort of lip-service worship to the gods, held festivals in their honor and made sacrifices to them (often human sacrifices). But, in general, the Greeks and Romans preferred simply to try to stay out of the gods' way and not attract their notice.

Take the Greek god Pan, for instance. He was the deity of the wildwood and of fields and flocks, and was believed to have the handsome face and body of a young man but the hindquarters of a goat. He was regarded as usually a most merry fellow, forever cavorting goatlike and tootling on his shepherd's pipes. But, as in most warm countries, it was the custom for people in Greece to lie down for an afternoon siesta—and so did Pan. Those Greeks who weren't likewise napping went about on tiptoe, for Pan's temper was as easily triggered as any other god's, and they feared his violence if he were rudely awakened. Small wonder that his name is still spoken in our word *panic*.

The Greeks, and consequently the Romans, believed in an afterlife, pleasant or dreadful, depending on how one had behaved on earth. The Greeks, and then the Romans, decided that the souls of good people went to the Elysian Isles—somewhere "way off to the west"—and that the bad souls went to an underground of eternal torment, supervised by the dread god Hades ("Pluto" to the Romans). Modern folk still use the word Hades or "the Plutonian depths" as an occasional synonym for Hell.

Beyond the bounds of the Mediterranean civilization, in the

far north of Europe, the Norse and Teutonic "barbarians" also had their crew of gods. Though the deities' names were different —and differed among the various northern bands—their allotted functions and their supposed personalities were so similar to those of the Greek and Roman gods that we are tempted to assume as true one of the following three theories:

—(*a*) both the southern and northern gods had originally been borrowed from those of the prehistoric wandering Indo-Europeans and had "developed" along similar lines,

—(*b*) an infrequent Greek or Roman explorer had traveled two thousand miles and more to what is now Germany and Scandinavia, and there had told stories of his native gods,

—(*c*) certain human needs, fears and hopes are universal, so that gods and devils are created to respond to these forces, sometimes quite independently, without "outside agitators," so to speak.

The Scandinavians and Germans had Woden (or Wodin or Odin) as their chief god, corresponding closely to Zeus and Jupiter in his sometimes jovial, sometimes ferocious, behavior. There was Tiw (or Tyr), the war god, equivalent to the Greek Ares and

Roman Mars. There was Thor (or Thunar), whose hammer struck the noise of thunder (he gave us that word)—exactly as did Greece's Hephaestos and Rome's Vulcan (who gave us the word *volcano*). There was Woden's wife Frigg (or Friga), goddess of love, the equivalent of Venus and Aphrodite—and many other gods and goddesses strikingly similar to those of the southern lands.

Of course, there were some variances in the far-apart religions. The northerners did not believe in an afterlife that rewarded good souls and punished bad ones. Almost all of their souls went to a rather grand and majestic underworld, presided over by a goddess named Hel, to live out their eternal afterlives in comfort. But the bravest warriors, when killed on the battlefield, had their souls collected by the warrior-demigoddesses called Valkyries. They were transported to the great, glittering hall of Valhalla, where Woden received them as heroes, and they feasted, fought, drank and made merry forever after.

However, long before they adopted this array of gods, whether invented or borrowed, the northerners had worshipped trees—simply because there were so many of them: thick, limitless forests covering all their lands. They continued to hold the trees sacred even after the advent of Woden, Frigg and company, and when they worshipped these gods they held their ceremonies in "holy groves" of trees. The sturdy and magnificent oak was their favorite. But, for their Midwinter Day rituals in which they implored the sun not to disappear entirely, the northmen turned their attention to the firs and pines—as encouragingly green as in summer—and bedecked them with beeswax candles, ribbons and other ornaments.

There was at least one highly advanced and sophisticated civilization of those days which did not swap any gods with other societies. That was China, and you might suppose that its aloofness was simply due to its remoteness, but that is not so. The Egyptian pharaohs wore silk imported from China, and other countries were engaged in sea trade with that nation a thousand years before Marco Polo made the famous first overland journey to the Far East. But the trading did not include gods, for China didn't have any. Oh, the Chinese paid some honor to their Adam-like "first-man," known in legend as P'an Ku, and to Sui Jen, the man who first learned how to make fire, allegedly by seeing a bird strike sparks when it pecked at a dry tree.

But when it came to worship, the Chinese of those times worshipped only their ancestors, whom they could hardly export, and they had no wish to import any of the Western gods. It was not until the spread of Buddhism that China began to admit missionaries of any new religion, and not until quite modern times that Chinese philosophies began to filter out to the peoples of the West.

And, of course, the Mediterranean civilizations, which set the course for most of our religions of today, had no knowledge at all of the religions practiced in the heart of Africa or in the totally unknown New World.

In these unexplored areas, the various African and American Indian tribes had also progressed intellectually to the point where they had elevated most of their former nature spirits to the status of nature gods, and in many cases had recognized the existence of a supreme god. The Angoni tribe of Africa, for example, worshipped many minor gods and one major god called Mulungu. Curiously, though, they did not give him credit for having created the earth, but for *running* it properly. His name would have translated as "Supervisor."

The Iroquois nation of the eastern part of North America had a religion that did not believe in praying for special favors, but in honoring all the gods for the favors they had *already* granted unasked. Their whole system of worship was a series of thanksgiving festivals, held periodically throughout the year. On one day or another, all the Iroquois tribes would foregather to thank "Our Mother the Earth," "Our Elder Brother the Sun," "Our Grandmother the Moon," "Our Grandfathers the Thunderers," and foremost of all, "Our Father the Creator of Everything." It is almost certain that the Iroquois tribe called the Wampanoag —of what is now Massachusetts—gave the Pilgrims the idea of celebrating their first Thanksgiving Day.

Another feature of the primitive African and Indian religions was cannibalism. However, no tribe ever killed, cooked and ate a human being just because they were hungry. This was a sacred rite. They would eat only enemies killed or captured in battle, and only those who had put up a fierce and brave fight. It was the victors' belief that by consuming part of such courageous opponents they would absorb some of the dead men's bravery, strength and cunning. Hence the victorious tribe usually ate only that part of a victim which they believed contained his virtues—to some it was his heart, to others his brain, his muscles, or whatever.

Similarly, they made an occasional ceremony of "eating their god"—that is, the totem animal, bird or fish which a tribe revered and had taken for its symbol. Ordinarily, they would never think of harming their totem. But now and then, presumably when the tribe had become weak or few in number, or low in morale, they would—with great rituals of apology, honor and thanks to the creature—kill and share among themselves the meat of the totem, in order to absorb some of the god's finer qualities and to bring themselves "closer to the god" in spirit. This ritual of eating one's deity has persisted—in a sublimated form, anyway—to the present day.

Except perhaps in some little-known corners of the world, all the gods and religions discussed in this chapter are long gone or suppressed. But traces of several of them still linger here and there. For example, the gods and goddesses of the northmen—Hel, Tiw, Woden, Thor, Frigg—have given us our names for Hell and for the days Tuesday, Wednesday, Thursday and Friday. The even more ancient worship of sun and moon gods has given us Sunday and Monday. The one-time Roman god of harvests, Saturn, gave us Saturday.

But there are deeper, not so obvious, aspects of the old religions which are still embedded in our culture, as we shall see when we examine modern religions. In short, not even the most savage and barbaric religions have ever vanished completely. The ancient Greeks were wrong when, at the coming of Christianity to their land, they cried out in lament: "Pán pámmegas téthnēke!" ("The great god Pan is dead!")

A
DEFIANCE
OF
DEVILS

Luther relates that he was alarmed when he heard a strange sound one night, until he perceived that it was only the Devil, and so went back to sleep.

— BERGEN EVANS

Many a man must have been considerably disappointed and a little annoyed when—after he had come to believe in gods and to pay them every kind of homage and reverence—his world did not burst gloriously into a Golden Age or revert to a Garden of Eden. As always, men were still plagued by disease, accident, hunger, thirst, misery, poverty, enemies, and death. A disillusioned man would jump to the easiest conclusion: his gods were not all-powerful.

Ever since he had begun to think and reason, man had been accustomed to seeing his world in black and white opposites, very seldom with shades of gray in between. For instance there was day opposed to night, light opposed to darkness, the weightless skies and the solid earth, male and female, life and death, good and evil. So it was only natural that he should imagine some force equal but opposite to the good gods—evil enemies whose delight it was to thwart the gods in every way, and especially when the gods tried to help their human worshippers.

Man had believed in good and bad spirits long before he ever conceived of gods. Later he disdained these spirits as poor weak things, compared to the gods, and demoted them. So now he was not about to start believing again in the power of evil spirits as being great enough to account for the bad things that kept happening in the world. No, it must be something far mightier than mere spirits opposing the gods. So he conceived of beings like the gods—except of course in personality and inclination— who were just as powerful (or maybe not *quite* as powerful) and just as dedicated to working ill as the gods were to working good. Thus came into being the "anti-gods." They have been known by many different names in different languages; today we usually refer to them as demons and devils.

But where did these devils and demons come from? And why were they so addicted to doing evil? Many explanations have been concocted, believed in, rejected and reinvented. The easiest, of course, was that everything in creation has its opposite—the day the night, the cold the heat, and so on—and therefore the forces of good must, by some "natural law," contend with the equal forces of evil.

So man imagined his demons as precisely the opposite of the gods in every respect. The gods were beings of light and beauty. The demons and devils skulked in the dark of night, which man has never ceased entirely to fear. The gods lived in the clean, high Heaven or atop a towering mountain. The anti-gods lived in the filthy Hell underground. (It is not too surprising that the early Christians, who lived in the subtropical Middle East, preached that Hell is a place of fiery furnaces and pits of boiling sulphur, all stoked to superheat by the demons. The men of the chilly north, when converted to Christianity and a belief in Hell, visualized it as a supercold place of eternal ice and snow.)

The gods were, in most societies, regarded as handsome—or at least as having familiar shapes: human form or the form of respected and friendly totem animals. Therefore, the demons must be hideously ugly, and unlike anything ever seen by mortal eyes. This assumption gave rise to the belief in all sorts of monstrous animals. Egypt had the mongrel leopard-hippopotamus-crocodile Devourer. The Greeks had the Chimera: a mixture of lion, goat and reptile. The Chaldeans had probably the most horrific; we don't know what they called it, but it had a dog's body, an eagle's claws for forefeet, the hindfeet of a lion, the venomous stinger tail of a scorpion, four great wings, and its head was a grinning, glaring human skull.

There is one invented animal which has figured as a demon monster in many countries, from England to China. It has been described in various ways, but we have come to think of it as the Chinese saw it: a head like a crocodile or a lion, batlike wings, a forked tongue, scaly body, barbed tail, sometimes horns—all in gaudy colors of gold and jade green and crimson. The one thing it had in common in all societies was that it supposedly breathed out either flames or a poison gas. We call this thing a "dragon," from an old Indo-European root *drk-on*, meaning simply "serpent." And in most countries the dragon seems to have been simply an exaggerated concept of the snake, whose killing power was feared by all peoples.

In China, however, the dragon seems to have been derived additionally from a quirk of topography. China's two greatest rivers, the Hwang Ho and the Yangtze, flow over flat clay plains, so they wind and meander like serpents, ever changing their courses. They are also subject to flash floods—in one recent flood, the Yangtze drowned more than a million people—so the rivers are rightly regarded as dangerous and unpredictable. That combination of serpentine movement and seemingly people-hating power could have inspired the idea of the Chinese dragon. Chinese artists could then have stylized the concept into that monstrous and spectacular beast which has become part of all the world's folklore.

Not all of man's demons and devils, however, were conceived as hideous animals; the great majority were more or less human in shape, though grotesquely magnified, grossly exaggerated, deformed or "uglified" in some other way.

The Greeks, for instance, had a slew of demonic beings. Among these were the Titans, a race of giants led by one Cronus; these had originally ruled the world and were overthrown by the late-comers Zeus and the other Olympian gods. Thenceforward the Titans became an underground race of demons, scheming and working against the gods.

Then there were the three Gorgon sisters, vultures with women's heads, except for the one named Medusa, who was a mortal and a lovely woman, provided one didn't look too closely: her glance would turn a man to stone, and her hair was a tangle of snakes. There were the Erinyes ("the Furies"), three ugly crones with batwings, the most ferocious of all demons. The Greeks were *so* afraid of incurring the wrath of the Furies that they never referred to them by that name, but fearfully called them the Eumenides ("the Kindly Ones").

The ancient Persians feared evil beings, of indescribable nature, called *daevas*. The Arabs feared the *djinn*, who could change shape at will, from pleasant-appearing human beings— even beautiful girls—to ugly, terrifying giants. The Norsemen feared an underground race called the *mara*, each of which had a different evil function to perform. One of the mara, for example, would crouch on a man's chest while he slept and smother him to death (hence our word "nightmare").

Similarly, Rome—and later, all Europe—believed in the male incubi and female succubi. The incubus was a demon who lay with women while they slept, and sapped their life strength; the succubus did the same to male sleepers. The ancient Irish had night demons called the *sidhe* (pronounced "shee"). One was the *leannain sidh* ("the lier-on" or "smotherer"), identical to the Norse night-mara. Another was the *bean sidh* ("banshee"), a hideous hag believed to wail and screech outside a house where Death was about to visit. Other, even more fright-prone cultures —especially in the Balkan countries—believed in such fearsome human demons (at least human at intervals) as the vampire and the werewolf, of which I'm sure I need give no description.

And everywhere in the world there were the baleful ghosts. Though many cultures have gone on believing that the ghosts of their friends and relatives visit them (usually in dreams) to give aid, comfort, advice or warnings, most societies regard ghosts as evildoers. They believe that the only "walking dead" are the souls of people evil in life, or who have become bitter after death because they died unjustly or too young, or by violence or suicide. Such ghosts could only harbor ill feelings against the living, and would wish to do them harm.

There was another source from which ancient societies drew their demons. This has been summed up in the saying that "the gods of the old religion become the devils of the new." Whenever a people devise a new religion or are converted to one by missionaries, or have it forced upon them by conquerors, they soon conclude (or, under duress, profess to believe) that heretofore they have mistakenly been worshipping "the evil ones." Now, shown the "true" religion of the "real" gods, they look back on the older gods as the "powers of darkness" from which they have been rescued. These rejected gods, though demoted to devils and demons, will of course sulk and lurk in their exile, and burst forth whenever they get the chance, to work havoc upon the people who have scorned them.

We will see many instances of the gods of the old religion becoming the devils of the new when, in later chapters, we examine the major religions of today. But here I will cite just one example. It is to be found in the architecture of Christianity's grandest cathedrals. The gargoyles, those stone figures which project at intervals from the cathedrals' eaves, usually serving as waterspouts to drain the rain from the roof, are in fact monuments to the old "pagan" gods displaced by the coming of Christianity.

The gargoyles are always carved into demon-like images, and they are meant to symbolize to the Christians that the old gods have been driven out from all places of worship and can nevermore come in. They are fixed immovably and miserably on the outside forever, watching their one-time worshippers serving the new religion. And they who once were gods are doomed to serve it, too, in the humiliating function of common rain gutters.

Early Christianity even conceived the notion of individual demons opposing individual angels and saints—or, if you prefer, the various angels and saints were assigned to vanquish certain demons which molested mankind. The archangel Raphael, it is said, personally wrestled with and overcame the demon Asmodeus for the soul of a maiden named Sara. According to the Roman Catholic Church, St. Apollonia is relied upon to cure toothache, St. Gervasius to cure rheumatism, St. Hubert to cure rabies, and a long chapter could be filled with other examples. In effect, though it is not doctrinally stated in so many words, each of these saints' particular task is to conquer the evil demon responsible for causing each of these afflictions.

Another Catholic saint who had his demon "opposite number" is even regarded with affection by Protestants. One Christmastime, in a village in the Bavarian Alps shared by Bavaria and Austria, I watched numerous local men dressed as the rotund, red-suited, white-whiskered St. Nicholas—or Santa Claus—troop from house to house carrying gifts for the children. All of a sudden, there swooped down from the mountains an equal number of men costumed hideously in great six-horned wooden masks, their gaping mouths lined with jagged teeth, and eye sockets eerily lit by flashlights inside. The men wore long goatskin robes and were wound all around with heavy chains and tremendous hollow iron balls. These "demons" came bellowing and howling, their iron globes booming as they bounced, and all this noise echoed and re-echoed from the snowy peaks roundabout.

Each of these monsters joined one of the Santa Clauses, and accompanied him on his rounds of the village houses. In this region—as it was explained to me—people still believed that only *good* children deserved to get gifts from St. Nicholas. The *bad* children still—in accordance with the original Santa Claus legend—merited only lumps of coal in their Christmas stockings and a good whipping to boot. These demons which had so surprised me were personations of Krampus, the "opposite" of St. Nicholas, and they carried and distributed the switches with which the naughty children were to be beaten.

Whatever the manner in which a society acquires its demons and devils, the people tend to rank them—as they do their gods—in a "chain of command," from the merely mischievous and annoying imps up to the really dreadful monsters. And those cultures which recognize one "chief god," master of all the others, do the same with their trolls, ghosts, goblins, animal monsters, ogres and other demons. One devil is set up as "commander-in-chief" of the whole demon population.

In Greece, as mentioned, the head devil was Cronus. In Babylonia, the reigning demon was a demoness, the Lady Nine, who enforced her rule with a pet dragon named Niamat. In Egypt, the chief anti-god was Set, who also kept a pet—the serpent Apap—and whose domain was not underground, but just as drear. Set ruled the wasteland of the Sahara, beyond the borders of the good god's green lands along the Nile River. To the northmen of Europe, Loki the Mischief-Maker was the most feared devil. Some African tribes believed that the chief of all demons was an immense, disembodied and nameless *stomach* that drifted through the forests, a few feet off the ground, seeking whatever (and whomever) it could devour.

In our western world today, say "demon" or "devil" and both Christians and Jews will immediately think of *The* Devil, or Satan. According to tradition, the Devil was originally one of the Lord God's best-loved angels, Lucifer ("the light-bearer," another name for the planet Venus). But Lucifer, in his pride, rebelled against God and so was cast out of Heaven. With a number of other dissident angels (who became his legion of demons), the fallen Lucifer "organized the underworld of Hell," you might say, and devoted himself to a career of tempting men into evil ways.

The ancient Hebrews gave him the name of Satan ("the adversary"), and Christianity has kept the name. In the Bible other names occur: Beelzebub ("lord of the flies," or plagues); Belial ("uselessness"); Asmodeus ("spirit of anger"), and several more, but it is not always clear whether these are alternate names for the Devil or names of his subordinate demons.

The Devil is mentioned frequently in the Bible, but makes only two personal appearances in its pages, and neither time is he described. So we do not know how the original believers in Satan visualized him, except for the remark in the Book of Revelations, "that old serpent, called the Devil"—and he was evidently also that serpent which tempted Eve to pluck the Garden of Eden's forbidden fruit. In later times, however, he was believed to assume many different shapes, each with a different personality. When not in disguise, he was supposed to be black all over, wearing horns, a barbed tail, and "cloven hooves" (obviously borrowed from the now-despised goatish god Pan).

Some fearful folks believed that the Devil appeared as a fiery-eyed fiend, kidnapping souls away to Hell. Others believed he could present himself as a most handsome, suave, smooth-talking gentleman, inspiring confidence instead of dread. (Which gave rise to the saying that "the loveliest trick of the Devil is to persuade you that he does not exist.") In this urbane disguise, Satan swindled good people into selling him their souls in exchange for some temporary wealth or other advantage during their lifetime. Anyway, what with the numerous different conceptions of Satan, it was only natural that men gradually loaded him with nicknames, ranging from respectful to contemptuous: from the Prince of Darkness and His Satanic Majesty to Old Nick and Old Scratch.

Well, we have seen how, for ages, men earnestly tried to excuse their gods for not producing an Instant Golden Age—by dreaming up demons and devils they could blame for all the misery that continued to plague their lives and the world in general. But there were, and still are, some people who take just the opposite view. They believe that the demons and devils are the more powerful supernatural beings, that evil will eventually tri-

umph over good, and they want to be on the winning side when the showdown comes. So—usually in secret, but sometimes brazenly in the open—these obstinate folk swear allegiance to the devils, demons and other "powers of darkness."

Devil-worship cults have existed in just about every known society and in every age—including our own. Groups of foolish and deluded people have tried the practice of black magic, witchcraft, "calling up demons" from Hell, and mocking religious worship of God by performing obscene parodies of prayer and church ceremonies. Such cults, whether determinedly vile or ludicrously moronic, have generally been short-lived, and there is not a jot of evidence that "selling his soul to the Devil" ever improved any cultist's life in the slightest. But the cults have had ill effects, not just for their practitioners, but for numerous innocent, godly folk as well.

For example, in the Middle Ages in Europe, there were probably never more than a handful of people who truly believed they were witches and could work magic with the aid of the Devil. But those few so outraged the Church that it began a campaign to stamp out witchcraft, and that campaign spread like wildfire. The word "fire" is deliberate—for uncountable hundreds of thousands of men, women and even tiny children were sent to the burning stake for no worse sin than that they were mentally retarded or addled by old age (and so behaved oddly), or simply because some malicious neighbor accused them of being witches.

To repeat, the mavericks who really thought they would "come out ahead" by backing the demons against the gods have never been more than an insignificant fraction of any society. Mankind would probably be extinct by now if the believers in good had not, everywhere and always, outnumbered the believers in evil. Most people, from primitive jungle tribesmen to the civilized and sophisticated folk of our own day, have given their allegiance to the God or gods of their religion. They have trusted in that belief to shield them from the powers of evil, have scoffed at the ridiculous devil worshippers, and at the same time have maintained what they consider a healthy fear and avoidance of the Devil's powers.

Staunch faith, a fast brush-off and, above all, laughter seem the best defense against Satan and those rattlebrained folk who keep coming up with "Satanic cults." The brilliant and famous sixteenth-century priest Martin Luther (already quoted in the heading to this chapter) once told a story which concerned a village where the Devil, passing through, decided to stop and bargain for a few souls. All the villagers were devout Christians but, instead of trying to banish Satan by solemn prayers or exorcism, they merely sneered and laughed at him until he fled with his barbed tail between his legs.

"When the Devil marked their contempt," said Luther, "he left off his game, and came there no more. He is a vain spirit, and cannot endure scorn."

STRANGE

BEINGS

AND

STRANGER

BELIEFS

These things seem wondrous, yet more wondrous I,
Whose heart with fear doth freeze, with love doth fry.

– ANONYMOUS (CA. 1600)

Here and there in the ancient world (and sometimes even today)
we find groups of people worshipping or paying tribute to, or at
least believing in such seemingly odd (or at least oddly named)
gods, demons, spirits and sprites as:

Baba of Poland
Green George among the European gypsies
Kaka of the Zuñi Indians
Hag of Wales
King Hop of Thailand
Coochie of the Australian Dieri
Ma of Armenia
Mama of Babylonia
Nut and Ptah of Egypt
Jack-in-the-Green of Olde England
The Norns of Scandinavia
Sir Charles M'Carthy (*British governor of Africa's Gold*

Coast, reverently eaten by the Ashanti tribe in 1824, that
they might absorb his wisdom and courage)
Dr. Iron-Beard of Germany
Gunputty and Punchkin of India, and so on.

Here and there we find people believing that many things
around them possess some sort of benevolent power or a helpful
spirit. These people worship or rely on, or at least try to stay on
friendly terms with, such good-luck bringers as:
Almonds in Phrygia
Rat's hair in South Africa
Orchids in Cambodia
Whales in Annam
Milkmen in India
Pepper in Java
Thorns in Bali
An enemy's knees in Sarawak
Crocodiles in Madagascar
A rabbit's foot or a four-leaf clover among us "moderns"
Red-haired men in Egypt, and so on.

Similarly, we find people believing that certain things around
them possess a malevolent power or spirit. So the people fear,
hate, dread, or at least try to avoid the possible evils connected
with:
Red-haired men in China
Dishwashing in Borneo
String among the Eskimos
Their own shadows in Indonesia
Eggshells in ancient Rome
Haircuts in Germany
Sweat in the New Hebrides
Their own toenails in Armenia
Falling down in Wales
Parrots' eggs in Dahomey
Mothers-in-law in Australia
Oatcakes rolling downhill in Scotland
Too-beautiful sunsets in Malaya

A broken mirror or the number 13 among us "moderns"
Singing in the shower or bath in Egypt, and so on

If you are interested in knowing more about those odd gods and other beings first mentioned, you can look them up in one or another of the larger encyclopedias. The odd *beliefs* would be harder to track down, so—especially since some are so bizarre you may think I made them up—I'd better explain them here. First, the "good" things:

In the ancient land of Phrygia (now a part of Turkey), the almond—the tree, the flower, the nut—was worshipped as the "father of all things," no doubt because the almond tree's delicate lavender-colored blossoms are the first harbinger of spring in that area. The flower blooms on the bare boughs even before the tree has sprouted leaves.

If you have ever tried to stone a rat to death, you will understand why the South African warrior twisted tufts of rat's hair among his own black curls whenever he was about to go into battle. It meant he would be as nimble as the rat when he had to dodge the enemy's spears.

In Cambodia, it was believed that if you saw an orchid growing on a tamarind tree you should run home, undress, reclothe yourself all in white, take a brand-new pot, climb the tree at noon, pluck the orchid, put it carefully in the pot . . . and let the pot fall from the tree and shatter on the ground. Then, if you brewed a tea of the orchid's leaves and drank it, you were forever after invulnerable to sickness or accident.

The Annamese of southeast Asia used to live mainly by fishing in the China Sea. They never had boats or gear strong enough to go whaling, but they considered the whale (actually a mammal) the father or chief of all fish. So, whenever a dead whale was washed ashore, the people of Annam gave it a solemn burial. The man who first found the carcass assumed the role of "next of kin," put on mourning clothes and directed the funeral rites. Perfume was sprinkled about, incense burned and firecrackers set off while the dead whale was burned. When nothing was left but its bones, these were interred in a specially built pagoda on the seashore. All of this, of course, was intended to persuade the other fish to let themselves be caught by the obviously honorable and reverent Annamese.

In all of India, cattle are held sacred, but especially so among the Todas who live in the south of that subcontinent. Since the cattle are so revered, so is their milk, hence so is the man who milks them and delivers the milk from door to door. Everyone of the Toda tribe falls prostrate when the milkman passes—even his own parents—and no one would dare refuse his slightest request. No human being, except another milkman, may touch him without permission, and he is often sought out for advice "from the gods."

In Java, a popular remedy for any number of ailments is to rub pepper deep into the tender flesh under the fingernails of the afflicted person. It hurts. But it hurts the "demon of disease" even more, and the demon supposedly departs in a hurry.

Every so often, a village in Bali will be so beset by ghosts that it will hold a mass ceremony of exorcism. Offerings of food are set out at a distant crossroads. Then the villagers rush through their streets waving torches, pounding on doors and shouting the Balinese equivalent of *scat!* and *shoo!* When, presumably, the ghosts have fled, found the food, and settled down to eat, the villagers return home, pile walls of thorn bushes around their houses and stay indoors for twenty-four hours, lighting no fires, and staying as still and silent as possible. The belief is that the ghosts return from their feast, find the village barred against them by the thorn bushes, and go elsewhere in search of a more hospitable town.

As mentioned earlier, many primitive peoples ate some selected portion of a killed or captured enemy to enhance their own qualities by adding those he showed in battle. They might eat his brain for cunning, his heart for bravery, and so on. The Dyaks of Sarawak used to boil and eat the skin of a slain enemy's knees in order to strengthen their own. Before you ask: I don't know—and no authority I have consulted can explain—why the Dyaks should have been so concerned about their knees.

The natives of the island of Madagascar would never kill a crocodile except in revenge for a friend killed by a crocodile. So, once a year, the Madagascans would gather at Lake Itasy and shout a proclamation: so-and-so-many of their people had been lost to the big amphibians in the past year, and the friends of the deceased were about to slaughter an equal number of crocodiles. This announcement supposedly warned all innocent crocodiles to keep out of the hunters' way, leaving only the evil ones to be killed; consequently, the lake would be inhabited only by "friendly" crocodiles.

In ancient Egypt, the god Osiris was believed to have red hair, perhaps because he was the son of the fiery sun god. Therefore, any other red-haired male—a rarity in Egypt—was much respected and pampered as he grew up. He was entertained by the pharaoh, given rich food and drink, a harem of women and anything else his heart desired. After he was well fattened and absolutely glowing with pleasure, he would be killed as a sacrifice to Osiris.

Now to explain some of the "not so good" things:

When Jenghiz Khan conquered China in the thirteenth century, one of his most ferocious, feared and hated generals was a redheaded man named Subatai. Red-haired men have been feared and mistrusted in China ever since.

The natives of Borneo used to earn their only cash income by collecting camphor, which oozes from the bark of the camphor tree and crystallizes in small grains, but then gradually evaporates into the air. So the Borneans, during the whole of a camphor-hunting expedition, would use a single big leaf as a plate for their every meal, and would never wash the encrusted food off that "dish," for fear that they would hasten the dissolving of the precious camphor grains they sought.

Eskimo boys used to be forbidden to play with string because, if they did, they might not be successful seal and walrus hunters when they grew up. Their string-bewitched fingers would get entangled in the harpoon line.

It was mentioned in an earlier chapter that many societies have regarded a person's shadow as a "fragment" of his soul. In certain islands of Indonesia, the natives made it a rule never to go out of their houses at noon, because by doing so—at the one time of day when they cast no shadow at all—they would risk losing their souls as well.

It has also been mentioned that in many places and at many times, any of a person's cast-offs—his hair, his nail clippings, even food left over from his meals—could be gathered up by a shaman or witch and used against him; for example, by being kneaded into a wax image of him which would then be tortured. In ancient Rome, a diner was especially careful to pulverize all the eggshells left after his meal. In Germany, a man gathered up all the scattered tufts from the barbershop floor after he'd had his hair cut. In the New Hebrides islands, a native was careful to keep himself well swabbed, so that not a single drop of sweat might fall and be collected by an enemy. In Armenia—and again don't ask me why—the people were particularly careful about picking up and burning their toenail parings.

In Wales, the people believed themselves peculiarly liable to the "falling sickness" (epilepsy). So they cured this—or better, avoided it—by taking a chicken to church and there going through a complicated rite which supposedly transferred the ailment to the fowl. As recently as 1855, the parish clerk of one

Welsh village told of seeing chickens staggering around his churchyard, afflicted by the falling-down fits that had been wished on them.

Any native of Dahomey unlucky enough to find a parrot's egg knew that he was doomed to die soon. So, when a Dahomeyan tribe grew tired of their chief's tyranny or decided that he was a weakling, his subjects would leave at his hut door a basket of parrots' eggs. The chief recognized the sign—and knew his duty. He would give his wives instructions to strangle him the next time he slept. (I can find no record of what happened to the tribesmen who found the parrots' eggs to give to the chief.)

We have all heard innumerable "mother-in-law jokes," and such jokes are prevalent all over the world—perhaps because originally mothers-in-law were no joke. They were feared and avoided. Among primitive tribes it was believed that when a man married, his wife's mother assumed some kind of magical and menacing power over him. The Australian aborigine, in particular, was so terrified of his mother-in-law that if even her shadow touched him he believed he would die. And so strong was his belief that he often did die, from no other apparent cause.

In Scotland, on the first of May—the first day of spring in those northern latitudes—it was the custom to hold great spring-welcoming ceremonies. One feature in many communities was the baking of big wheel-shaped oatcakes, which were to be rolled down a hill, a custom related to our Easter egg-rolling. If a cake broke as it rolled, the baker of that one could expect to die or suffer some other dire misfortune during the following year.

In Malaya, as in many other parts of the world, it was believed that one's soul could leave the body and go wandering about on its own. And the Malayans evidently believed their souls to be a bit dim-witted; they were sure that any change in a person's appearance would confuse the returning soul. If it didn't immediately recognize its body, it would drift away again and maybe never return. So the Malayans refrained from wearing any kind of facial make-up or warpaint—and even took care to hide whenever there was an especially colorful sunset, for fear that the rays would "paint" their faces and make them unrecognizable to their souls.

To this day, even intelligent Egyptians will not make any unnecessary noise while using their bathrooms. (For that matter, only the wealthier—and therefore *presumably* intelligent—Egyptians can afford a bathroom.) The Egyptians still believe in a multitude of spirits, one of whom, named Gada, seems to do nothing but live in people's bathrooms and nurse his exceptionally irritable temper. Anyone who sings in the shower or whistles, or whatever, may not get out of that bathroom intact.

There have been many other odd gods, beliefs and religious customs besides those already cited. My choice for one of the most beguiling forms of worship ever known was that found by Marco Polo in a tribe on the island of Java. There a person worshipped, all day long, the first object he or she laid eyes on when awakening each morning. Of course, in thirteenth-century Java, this object might have been a bird, butterfly, blossom, or the person's mate—and the Javanese are exceptionally beautiful people. Such a belief would not be so enchanting today, when (even in Java) a person's first sight might be of a motorcycle or a TV antenna.

The Indians living along the shore of ancient Peru worshipped the fish, which they caught in great abundance, and which therefore were the mainstay of their diet. They believed that each species had its "father fish" in what they called The World Above, and that this fish-god took care to provide them with a plenitude of his sons and daughters. Thus, laughable as it may seem to us today, the god of one Peruvian fisher tribe was The Great Sardine.

The natives of Madagascar worshipped or feared (or both) a great number of nature gods. But they did believe in one supreme deity who ruled over all the rest. When Christian missionaries came to the island in 1820, most Madagascans refused conversion to belief in Jehovah and Jesus—much preferring their older deity, the beautifully named Andriamanita, which means "the fragrant one." Their queen, Ranavalona, finally evicted the missionaries and summarily executed all her subjects who had turned Christian. (Queen Ranavalona was always high-handed. At one time, she pronounced a decree that *none of her subjects should appear in her dreams,* and executed any who did.) It was not until after her death in 1861 that Christianity returned to Madagascar . . . and soon the great god Fragrant One was dead.

The ways in which people have worshipped their deities have often been wildly at variance in different places and at different times, or at different places at the same time, or sometimes simultaneously within a single society. Today, for instance, Jewish men wear their hats when worshipping in a synagogue, believing it reverent to keep their heads covered before God. Perhaps just down the block, men of a Christian congregation doff their hats at the church door, believing it reverent to uncover their heads before the same God.

The ancient Hebrews buried their dead—all but the vilest criminals, who had to suffer the humiliation of having their bodies cremated. The ancient Maya buried their dead—all but the highest nobles, who merited the honor of having their bodies cremated. Today, Protestant Christians usually obey a dying man's last wish as to the disposal of his body—cremation or burial. Roman Catholic Christians disapprove of cremation, as it leaves no body to be resurrected entire on Judgment Day. All Christians used to insist that their dead be buried with the feet toward the east, so they might arise the more readily at that Last Trumpet (to come, presumably, from where the sun rises). Muslims are always buried with their heads toward the Holy City of Mecca in Saudi Arabia.

Like the Catholics of today, many ancient religions believed that the body should be buried entire, and even preserved against decay—or at least the bodies of kings, high priests and ranking nobles. We are all familiar with the Egyptian practice of mummifying the bodies of such aristocrats. Not so well known is the fact that other societies likewise mummified their dead. The Incas of Peru preserved their nobles' bodies, and even continued to carry them on litter-chairs in religious processions for years or decades after their death. One tribe of East Africa used to bury a dead person, then light a long-burning fire atop the grave to bake the body to a mummy.

As we know, many early societies also buried with a dead person all the goods and comforts he might need in the next world, or upon his return to this one on some future Resurrection Day. In Asia Minor, China and Egypt, the higher-ranking dead were buried with valuable objects of gold, silver, jade and porcelain. Later and more sophisticated societies began to consider this a waste of their treasures. The Chinese, for instance, later interred their dead with paper images of the appropriate supplies: paper chickens for food, counterfeit money, even life-sized servants, soldiers and horses made entirely of paper. Since the souls of the dead would need only the "souls" of their belongings in the next world (or so reasoned the Chinese) good imitations were as likely to serve them as objects of value that the living could better use.

The prehistoric Toltecs of Mexico sacrificed small, beautiful creatures to their gods: butterflies and quail. The late-arriving Mexica (or Aztecs), Tlaxcalteca and other tribes sacrificed their fellow humans, captured from each other. When there was no political or territorial squabble to justify a war, two or more tribes would arrange to fight a "Flower War"—just as fierce as any other combat, but with no object of conquest—purely to capture victims from the opposing side whom they could use as sacrifices to their gods.

If that sounds coldblooded, consider the sacrificial methods used by the Chinese, even well into the past century. They put their victims to death with ingenious tortures—The Death of a Thousand Cuts, The Death of a Thousand Caresses, and others—all of which can be better imagined than described. But the sacrificial victims were selected from among criminals, traitors and such, who presumably deserved these cruel, slow deaths.

India's sacrifices were even more brutal. From ancient times, India has had the least compassion and regard for human life of any society known—possibly because the country is so overcrowded with people that any number can be spared. The British occupation of India, in 1757, had put an end to most of the more gruesome practices. But the withdrawal of Britain's civilizing influence in 1947 has enabled some Indian sects to return (though usually in secret) to some of those practices. And the old-time sacrifices, as often as not, involved totally innocent victims—not criminals or prisoners of war—sometimes even the friends or relatives of those who butchered them.

The Khonds of the state of Bengal sacrifice to their earth goddess Tari Pennu to ensure good crops. The Khonds' main crop is turmeric (which yields a deep reddish-yellow dye), and the Khonds have always believed that their turmeric would get its best possible color from an infusion of human blood. Other tribes in other parts of India have sacrificed for other reasons, but the rituals always required the spilling of human blood—and generally in the most gruesome way imaginable.

A tribe would take up a public subscription, then buy an infant from one of the tribe's poorer families. This child would be carefully tended and well fed during the growing-up years. It might even be given a house and land, a wife or husband (also a paid-for victim-to-be). For some ten or twelve days before the time for the sacrifice, the victim (and mate, if there was one) would be indulged in revelry, fine food and fun. All the other tribesmen would try to pluck one of the victim's hairs for luck or even beg that he or she would simply *spit* on them.

Then all the fun and festivity would end, and the victim would be put to death in one of several different ways. Sometimes the human sacrifice would be tied up and dragged through the fields, while a horde of his fellow villagers ran alongside with knives and hatchets, hacking bits off him until he was dead. One village had a carved wooden elephant, fixed to revolve on a post. The victim was tied to the elephant's extended trunk and the elephant was spun like a merry-go-round, while a circle of villagers stood hacking and jabbing with their blades as the victim whizzed past them.

Another village made a mound of earth and built a fire around it. The victim was tightly bound and laid atop the mound. Then his fellows poked him with burning sticks as he rolled up and down the mound, in and out of the fire, shrieking and weeping. In this mode of sacrifice, the worshippers kept the victim alive as long as possible, because the more tears he shed the more rain there'd be during the growing season. As soon as the victim was dead, or sometimes even while he was still alive, his body would be minced into tiny chunks so that every farmer would have a bit of flesh to plant with his crop.

Another grisly practice was that of headhunting—not only among several of the bloodthirsty tribes of India, but also among the Karens of Burma, numerous South Pacific islands, throughout Africa, and to this day in the more remote jungle parts of South America.

All headhunters took up this practice because they believed the head was the part of the body that contained the soul. Some headhunters were merely cannibals, and ate an enemy's head to absorb its soul-qualities. But most headhunters had a more sophisticated concept. The enemy's head contained his soul; therefore, if the victor carried the head home with him, the soul was his prisoner. Therefore, when he (the victor) died, he would have the soul as his servant in the next world. Therefore, the more enemy heads he collected, the more leisurely and luxuriously he himself would live in the next world. In many African tribes, this collecting of enemies' heads was known as "touching meat," and the tribes' girls would refuse to marry a suitor until he had "touched meat" at least once.

But headhunting has not been confined to savages. In civilized Europe, as late as 1912, the various communities of Montenegro, then an independent kingdom, were forever feuding among themselves. And the Montenegrins happily cut off and carried home the heads of slain opponents. But then came the full-scale Balkan War of 1913, and the Montenegrins were drafted into service as soldiers. They found it rather inconvenient to carry whole heads around with them, so, during that war, whenever they slew an enemy, they would content themselves with merely taking his nose, along with his upper lip and its mustache (which every Balkan soldier wore).

But even with headhunters, as with so many other cultures, reasons of expediency began to influence their religious customs. When the first explorers of New Zealand found the native Maori huts hung with shrunken heads, they bargained for them—offering trinkets and gewgaws that the Maoris couldn't resist, even though it meant a loss of servants in the next world—and the explorers took the horrid things back to Europe as souvenirs.

These "pickled heads," as they were then called, became items of trade as curios and gifts. More and more traders descended on New Zealand, demanding heads and offering higher and higher prices. The Maoris shrugged, left their everyday pursuits to concentrate on headhunting, and very nearly exterminated themselves collecting each other's heads not for spiritual reasons, but for pure profit.

MEN

(AND

WOMEN)

LIKE

GODS

That's what makes us the unique animal, we want to know why and try to find out. We even try to discover why we want to know why, though of course we never will.

— REX STOUT

I have already told in a previous book, *March of the Heroes,* how many men of ancient days, particularly in Greece, led such heroic lives on earth that after their death the people believed they had been elevated to Mount Olympus to dwell with the gods. So they were themselves worshipped as gods. Among these deified Greek heroes were the great warrior Ajax, the sublime musician Orpheus, and the master physician Asklepios.

Other Greek heroes had an easier chance of being transmuted into gods, for they were the demigod offspring of a god and a mortal woman, or a goddess and a mortal man. These included Herakles, son of Zeus and the mortal Alcmene; Perseus, son of Zeus and the mortal Danaë; and Achilles, son of the sea goddess Thetis by the mortal Peleus. The notion of demigods being born of the union of gods and mortals appears to have been borrowed by the Greeks (as they had borrowed so many ideas) from another religion, that of the ancient Sumerian civilization of the Middle East.

In Sumer, each city had its supreme god, who was provided with a palace even grander and more richly furnished than that of the city's ruler. The god was given a "chief wife," called his *entu*—usually the city ruler's sister or daughter—and this foremost wife was forbidden to associate with any mortal man. However, the god was also provided with a whole harem of secondary wives, called *sal-me*. Though they were ceremoniously "married" to the god and lived in his palace, they were not prevented from casual matings with any men who took their fancy. And any children born to them were regarded as "children of the god." There is no record of any of the *sal-me* offspring ever becoming gods themselves, or even carving an heroic reputation for themselves. But when the Greeks took over this concept of demigod children, they elaborated on it—and the children of god fathers or goddess mothers inevitably, in Greece, grew up to be first heroes and then gods in their own right.

Many another ancient society has elevated its mortal heroes and mortal kings to godhood, sometimes while they were still alive. The prophets of many newborn religions, while seldom proclaiming themselves gods and perhaps never even called gods by their followers, have nevertheless been revered and worshipped as adoringly as any long-recognized god. Even lesser divinities, such as angels and saints—though they may have lived on earth as mortal men at one time—have come in for their share of near-godlike worship.

In Africa, the primitive Hottentots (they called themselves the Khoi-Khoin) have long worshipped the once-mortal Heitsi-Eibib. He was one of their tribal warriors who, though frequently killed in battle, was believed to come back to life whenever the tribe needed his fighting prowess. And so, though he has evidently ceased returning to life, he is still considered the Khoi-Khoin's chief god.

In the African nation of Buganda (now the Republic of Uganda), all the greatest gods were really ghosts, since all of them were believed to have lived on earth as men in earlier times. Each clan took for its chief deity the spirit of its first ancestor. And every time a tribal king died, there was a great ceremony held—involving the sacrifice of hundreds of his subjects—while the king's soul was translated from mortality into godhood.

In ancient days, Japan worshipped a number of nature gods and goddesses (the religion was called Shinto), but gradually came to conceive of the sun goddess Amaterasu as the supreme deity. And as the various, formerly feuding little kingdoms of the islands slowly united into the single nation of Japan, under a single emperor, the people decided that that emperor had been born of the sun goddess. Today, Emperor Hirohito of Japan is still believed to be a direct descendant of Amaterasu, and the flag of Japan still bears only the single, stark symbol of the red sun on a field of pure white.

Being a living god was not always a joy to the Japanese emperors, however. By the twelfth century, the emperor was considered too holy to concern himself with anything as trivial as ruling the country. That was left to the mortal (and tyrannical) nobles called *shoguns*. The emperor was merely trotted out for public appearances once in a great while, and on such occasions his actions were rigidly constricted. He could not, for instance, look anywhere but straight ahead. If he turned his glance, he would cause an earthquake somewhere in the direction in which he looked. Even in private, he was shackled by religious rules and regulations. His hair and nails could be cut only when he was asleep. Anything he touched became instantly sacred and unusable by any lesser person. He had to eat from new dishes at every meal, and these were destroyed immediately afterward. Consequently, the emperor dined off cheaper dinnerware than did any poor peasant in his land.

Other men, far from finding the idea of being a living god unpleasant to contemplate, have tried to proclaim themselves as such. One was Empedocles, a Sicilian philosopher of the fifth century B.C. and probably the wisest man of his time. He theorized correctly that everything in the universe is composed of certain elements, merely in different combinations, and that all change (cold to heat, firewood to ashes, etc.) is caused by the motion of those elements. This was basically a correct foreshadowing of the molecular theory of change still held by scientists today.

Empedocles also theorized that the earliest creatures on earth were a rabble of freaks: man-beasts, beast-men, humans of no sex, humans who combined both sexes in one body, etc. Only those adapted to life and to the reproduction of their own kind—such as the oppositely sexed men and women—survived and multiplied to populate the planet. In this, Empedocles was anticipating Darwin's "survival of the fittest" theory of evolution, more than 2,200 years before Darwin.

Anyway, having settled these weighty matters to his own satisfaction, Empedocles decided that since he was the only man who knew how the world was created, he himself must rank with the gods who had created it. Perhaps all his brainwork had overloaded his brain, for Empedocles now went about claiming that he could make the wind blow as he wished, the rain to fall or the sun to shine, that he could banish illness and old age and raise the dead. Somewhat pathetically—since no one ever took him seriously—Empedocles even recited to his fellow citizens of Agrigentum a poem he wrote in his own honor, including the following lines:

> "Wherever I go, the people crowd and worship pay,
> And thousands follow, to learn the Better Way."

Sometime around A.D. 1500, when the land of Burma was firmly Buddhist in religion, one of Burma's petty kings, envying the worship paid to Buddha, decided to have himself proclaimed a god. He first tried doing this by slaughtering any subject who refused to say he was a god. This didn't convert the devout Buddhists, and the king was rapidly running out of subjects, so he tried a new tack. He would imitate Buddha in every way, and thereby become the equal of the long-dead Buddha, hence be adored as was Buddha. So he gave up his crown, retired from his palace, abandoned his queen, family and harem of lesser wives, and went off to lead a life of meditation, fasting and self-denial (though he did this in a quite luxurious pagoda he had had built for the purpose). He surrounded himself with sage Buddhist bonzes (monks), to whom he incessantly preached that he was the Buddha reborn. But the bonzes would have none of this nonsense. Besides, the ex-king—even in these comfortable quarters—found himself missing the fine foods, pomp, regalia, fearful respect and iron rule he had formerly enjoyed. So he renounced his ambition to be a god, returned to his palace, donned his

crown, executed several hundred more of his subjects out of mere peevishness . . . and today even his name is forgotten.

Not all of those who claimed to be gods or were willy-nilly proclaimed gods after their death lived in ancient times or primitive societies. Many such have emerged in modern civilizations.

For instance, in the south of France in the twelfth century, there arose a sect called the Albigenses. One of their beliefs was that every human being was God, or at least a fragment of God represented in the flesh. So the Albigenses worshipped, not an abstract god up in Heaven or a more tangible god in Nature—but each other. Every single individual—man, woman and child—of the Albigenses was entitled to worship, prayer and reverence from all the others.

The New Testament's Book of Revelations, written about A.D. 95, prophesied that sometime in the future there would appear "a great wonder . . . a woman clothed with the sun, and the moon under her feet." This woman was to give birth to "a man child, who was to rule all nations with a rod of iron." That child was to be "caught up unto God, and to his throne"—another Jesus, in other words. Well, that "great wonder" of a woman finally appeared—or said she did—in England, seventeen centuries later. Her name was Joanna Southcott. She had been a housemaid in a remote Devonshire village, and a devout Methodist until she began having supernatural visions in 1792 which convinced her that she was no mere mortal. She started dictating prophecies in rhyme (she had to dictate, as she could neither read nor write), her name and fame began to spread, and she collected a band of followers. She moved to London and eventually gathered a sect numbering nearly 150,000, each of whom she "sealed to her" for a fee, which made her quite wealthy.

Early in 1814, at the age of 63, unmarried and a virgin, she announced that she was the woman spoken of in Revelations, and that on October 19 of that year she would give birth to that splendiferous son. Upon which, she went into a most convincing trance and never came out of it. Neither did any child. Joanna Southcott died of brain disease. She left a locked box which was not to be opened until Great Britain faced some dire crisis, from which it would be saved by the box's contents. The Southcott cult languished and its followers drifted away. But there were still enough of them left in 1928 (when Britain was in no particular crisis) to open the box out of mere curiosity. Says a history book, "It was found to contain nothing of any interest at all."

In the seventeenth century, also in England, was founded the Society of Friends, which still thrives. It is, indeed, one of the Christian sects which most closely adhere to the original, simple teachings of Jesus Christ. However, at its beginning, the Society of Friends was sneered at by other denominations, and its members were derisively called "Quakers" because they often, during worship services, visibly trembled at "feeling the spirit of the Lord."

Splinter groups began to break away from the Society of Friends, each of these having different ideas of how they should worship. One of the groups—whose members got so ecstatic when worshipping that they didn't just quake but danced, pranced and went into convulsions—became scornfully known as the "Shakers." They called themselves The United Society of Believers in Christ's Second Coming, and their leader was a woman, Ann Lee. Daughter of a blacksmith, married to a blacksmith

(Abraham Stanley, but Ann insisted on retaining her maiden name), Miss Lee, like Joanna Southcott, could neither read nor write. But she was an effective leader and a powerful speaker. After she had been jailed in England for her noisy public preaching, Miss Lee led two other women and six men to America in 1774, where her Shaker movement really boomed. Shaker communities sprang up—consisting of 30 to 90 "families" apiece—from the Atlantic seaboard as far west as the frontier Indiana. Miss Lee demanded that her followers keep two foremost commandments: 1. A belief that the Lord God was actually dual in identity; the male half of God was Jesus Christ; the female half of God was Ann Lee (called by the Shakers "Mother Ann" or "Ann of the Word"). 2. The men and women of Shaker "families" should not live—or at least go to bed—together. (Miss Lee's husband Abraham seems to have conveniently disappeared about this time.)

By 1874, a hundred years after their arrival in America, and ninety years after Mother Ann's death, the Shakers were at their peak in membership, with 58 communities containing some 2,500 inhabitants, scattered across the United States. But Mother Ann's rule of separating the men and women almost automatically doomed the movement—for no children were born to sustain it, and not enough converts joined to replace the dying off of the elders. Within another hundred years, the Shakers would be extinct.

Shakerism had one curious and tragic side effect, however. About 1870, a teen-aged Paiute Indian boy named Wovoka was working for a white family of Shakers. They gave Wovoka the "white name" of Jack Wilson and evidently initiated the youngster into their sect—or at least let him watch their ceremonies. When Wovoka went back to his tribe in Nevada, he took along his new religion—or what he understood of it. Soon he had his whole tribe dancing what he called the Ghost Dance, wearing the white Ghost Shirts he had introduced, falling into trances and fits just as the Shakers did.

Then, during an 1887 eclipse of the sun (which seems always to have deranged primitive peoples), Wovoka claimed he had seen a vision. The gist of it was that if all Indians followed his new religion, there would come a time when the earth would die and then be reborn with no whites but only red men on it (including all the past dead) who would live forever, free from disease, misery and death. It was not long before the Ghost Dance religion had spread throughout Indian tribes from the Pacific Coast to the Great Plains, and Wovoka was known, even to whites, as "The Indian Messiah."

But different tribes variously interpreted the new religion. The Sioux, for example, firmly believed that their Ghost Shirts were bulletproof—and this led to the last major clash between Indians and whites in the United States. In 1890, the U.S. 7th Cavalry rounded up a band of two hundred Sioux braves, squaws and children, and herded them toward a South Dakota reservation. When they got as far as Wounded Knee Creek, the cavalry commander ordered all the Indians disarmed. One brave, trusting in the invulnerability of his Ghost Shirt, pulled a gun, shot and wounded an Army officer. Instantly, the entire troop of cavalry opened fire—wiping out every one of the two hundred Sioux in minutes. The massacre at Wounded Knee was the blackest day in Indian-white relations, and has rankled ever since in the conscience of both red and white men. It also put an end to Wovoka-Jack Wilson's Ghost Dance religion and his own godhood. He died forlorn and forgotten in 1932.

Still another new-religionist was Joseph Smith. As a boy on a New York farm, he was prone to seeing visions, and in 1822, when he was eighteen, he claimed to have been visited by an angel named Moroni, who told him of some golden tablets inscribed with prophetic writings. These, said Moroni, had been hidden by one of the "lost tribes of Israel" which, in biblical days, had wandered as far as New York State and lived there until the year 600.

In 1827, young Smith claimed that the angel had finally shown him these "books of the prophet Mormon," and had helped him translate the secret writings. The angel Moroni also conferred "priesthood" on Smith and a friend, Oliver Cowdery, after which Smith dictated the contents of the tablets to Cowdery (no one but Smith ever got a look at the alleged golden tablets), and this, *The Book of Mormon*, became the guidebook for Smith's Church of Jesus Christ of Latter-Day Saints.

Smith rapidly gained a following, but he and his "Mormons," as they are popularly known, also suffered many setbacks—especially after Smith had another vision, in which he was instructed to wed as many wives as he wanted. This became a doctrine of the new religion, practiced by practically all the Mormons, and a doctrine which made other people hate, despise and persecute them. It even impelled a lynch mob in Illinois to murder prophet Joseph Smith and his brother Hyrum.

Smith has never really been revered as a god, but rather as a martyr. In fact, his role in Mormonism was considerably overshadowed by the succeeding prophet, the flamboyant Brigham Young (27 wives, number of children still not ascertained), who led the Mormons on a long and heroic march to the shores of the Great Salt Lake, where they founded the state of "Deseret" (meaning "honeybee," according to *The Book of Mormon*), and made the barren land bloom.

For a long time, the thriving Mormoms discouraged any other settlers. In fact, they massacred a party of 140 innocent emigrants whose wagon train was merely passing through en route to California—and Deseret narrowly avoided being besieged by the U.S. Army as a result. The Mormons guard their privacy and their right to worship as they please, but in 1890 they unbent enough to repeal the "vision" allowing them multiple wives, and thus their state of Deseret was finally permitted to join the Union as the state of Utah.

Just as Smith and Young were revered only as prophets and not as literal gods, so have all later presidents of the Latter-Day Saints been regarded. Each new president-prophet is elected only on the death of his predecessor, to serve all *his* life long. Though technically he rules with the aid of two priest-counselors and a Council of Twelve (the Apostles), the president is the supreme authority for the more than 3,000,000 Mormons, and his word is "the word of God."

The next (and still growing) religion to be founded was the work of a woman, Mary Baker. In delicate health all her life long, she nearly died after being severely injured in a fall on an icy sidewalk in Lynn, Massachusetts, in 1866. Confined to what she assumed was her deathbed, she read in her Bible the passage (Matt. 9:2–8) wherein Jesus commands a bedridden man to "Arise, take up thy bed, and go unto thine house"—and the man does so. Almost overnight, Mary Baker was out of bed—hale, hearty and healthier than she had ever been. (She was 45 years old then, and lived to be 89.)

Convinced that only God, Jesus, and their laws and teachings were "realities" and that disease, accidents and other miseries were "unrealities" caused by human "error," Mary Baker sat down to interpret the Bible in terms of "modern science." (The late nineteenth century was very science-minded.) Her commentary on the Bible she entitled *Science and Health* (it was later subtitled *With a Key to the Scriptures*) and this became the textbook for her Church of Christ, Scientist, which she founded in Boston in 1892.

Her new religion was an instant success, attracting believers in scores and hundreds from its very beginning. Mary Baker, already once widowed and once divorced, married one of her earliest converts, Asa Eddy. Almost every Christian Scientist since has referred to her respectfully as "Mrs. Eddy." But some—noting the concidence of her first name, and the fact that her first Boston church is always called the "Mother Church"—are inclined to call Mrs. Eddy even more reverently "Mother Mary." As of this writing, the Mother Church has spawned nearly 3,500 branch churches in 58 countries.

The basic tenet of Mrs. Eddy's religion is that any illness or other bothersome aspect of life can be done away with through the Christian Science application of proper "knowledge of the law of God, the law of Good." Mrs. Eddy elaborated on this, in copious detail, in more than a dozen later books. And the laws and rules she set down for the governing and functioning of her church—even the slightest details of the worship ceremony—are still most rigidly adhered to. One of the rules is that no Christian Science church shall have a pastor. Instead, two "readers" alternately intone passages from the Bible and from Mrs. Eddy's *Science and Health*, giving equal time to each authority.

Mrs. Eddy also established a number of Christian Science

periodicals which are still published, monthly or weekly. At the age of 87, she started the *Christian Science Monitor,* which today is one of the world's most respected and widely read daily newspapers, although—Mrs. Eddy specified this—it is "free from sensational and scandalous news." It is also, even in its obituary columns, free from the words, *die, died* and *death.* Death is an unreality. Christian Scientists *pass.*

THE

GOD(S)

OF

THE JEWS

I now have the right to do right, to do justice, to do good, to serve humanity, to help the needy, to heal the sick, to strive for peace, to seek after truth, to fight oppression, to liberate all mankind from bondage . . .

— TRADITIONALLY READ BY EVERY JEWISH BOY OF THIRTEEN AT HIS BAR MITZVAH (COMING OF AGE)

According to my desk calendar, I am writing this in the year 1975—that is, the 1,975th year since the supposed date of the birth of Jesus Christ. I could also say that I am writing this in the year 5735, for, according to the Jewish calendar, this is the 5,735th year since the supposed Creation of the world, from which the Jews date their earliest ancestors, Adam and Eve. Dates and traditions aside, it is certain that of all the major religions still observed in our world, the oldest is Judaism—the worship of one and only one Lord God Almighty—which evolved in the Fertile Crescent of Africa and the Middle East long before any other of today's religions were born.

The Fertile Crescent is a long, broad stretch of land at the eastern end of the Mediterranean Sea. It arcs from Egypt's Nile River delta northward into the Middle East, through what are now Israel, Jordan and Lebanon, then east through Syria and southeast down the lush valleys of Iraq's Tigris and Euphrates

Rivers (according to legend, the site of the long-ago Garden of Eden) to the Persian Gulf.

Fertile in more than crops and herds and populations, the Crescent has long been fertile in ideas, inventions and discoveries. It was the seedbed of all our modern Western civilizations (transmitted to us partly by the later, ever-borrowing Greeks and Romans). Surrounded by bleak deserts and open sea, the Fertile Crescent has long been a battleground for numerous peoples, each wanting possession of it, or a part of it. At one time or another, in the ancient days, it was the home of such people as the Sumerians, Babylonians, Phoenicians, Assyrians, Persians, Hyksos, Hittites, Philistines, Israelites, Judeans and others.

The Sumerians, Hyksos, Persians and Philistines appear to have been branches of those far-wandering Indo-Europeans who have kept cropping up throughout this book and in all parts of the ancient world. The Egyptians spoke a Hamitic language—which is to say, they were supposedly the descendants of Noah's son Ham. But those other peoples listed in the paragraph above were Semites—supposedly the descendants of Noah's other son, Shem—and all spoke variants of the same Semitic tongue.

During those long ago ages, the various peoples fought and vanquished one another, allied with one another, absorbed one another, intermarried with one another, until today it would be difficult to differentiate among their descendants. And no matter how much they fought, no matter which society was on top at the time, all freely swapped and adopted myths, legends, heroes, gods and religions from one another. This is provable just from a quick look at some of the stories most cherished in Jewish tradition.

In Genesis, the very first book of the Old Testament, we see the Lord God creating Adam from "the dust of the ground." Biblical scholars have demonstrated that this book of Genesis could not have been written before 850 B.C. However, more than eleven centuries before that, the Babylonians were saying that their "Mother-of-All," the goddess Aruru, had made "the first man" from a lump of clay.

Also in Genesis, we learn of the Great Flood, and of how Noah, his family and all those two-by-two animals survived it.

Again, the Babylonians' writings of eleven centuries earlier tell of a similar flood, which the hero Ut-Napishtim survived by building a great boat, into which he crammed not only animals but humans—artisans of every trade—plus tools and weapons.*

Exodus, the second book of the Old Testament, also written no earlier than 850 B.C., introduces us to Moses as a baby, lying in a cradle made of bulrushes hidden among the reeds of Egypt's Nile River, where he was found and adopted by the pharaoh's daughter. Moses lived and died some five hundred years before that account was written. But, another five hundred years before Moses was *born*, King Hammurabi of Babylonia was telling how he, as a baby, had been found floating in a basket in a drainage ditch, and had been adopted by a gardener. There are numerous other Jewish traditions which have been borrowed from the Babylonians, and from other cultures, too, as we shall see.

During the earliest centuries, the Fertile Crescent was occupied by wandering nomads: hunters and herders. Then, sometime before the Great Flood, the Indo-European Sumerians settled in the Middle East as farmers and, after the flood, began to raise communities, towns, even cities, until they had built the first urban *civilization* in that area. About the same era, farther down the Crescent in Africa, Egypt's civilization was similarly evolving. Sometime around 3000 B.C., the first Semitic tribes began infiltrating into Sumer. Sheepherders and goatherds, they apparently

---

* The Great Flood persists in the folklore of innumerable societies because it really happened. At the culmination of the last Ice Age, the canyons of the Caucasus and Himalaya Mountains were clogged with glaciers: immense, deep rivers of ice. As these ice rivers slowly crunched their way through the mountain passes, they piled up in front of them—like bulldozer blades—towering heaps of loose dirt and rocks. When the Ice Age passed and the world began to warm again, the glaciers slowly melted, and for a long, long time their waters were contained by the damlike moraines of piled-up rubble. But finally, about 3500 B.C., the moraines could stand no longer, and the water burst out like a tidal wave. From the Caucasus Mountains the floodwaters swept across the Fertile Crescent, flooding every river and making it overflow its banks. From the Himalayas, the water poured down into India and China. The Great Flood did not, as God threatened in the Book of Genesis, "destroy all flesh . . . and every thing that is in the earth." It did, however, drown a good many people, destroyed much property, and made such an impression on the minds of men that they were still making myths about it thousands of years later—and believing them to this day.

came from the torrid deserts of South Arabia, for they brought with them several gods which would seem to have originated there.

These gods included Shamash, the sun god; Nabu, the god of wisdom; and Ashtar, the god (a male, you'll note) of the planet Venus. The Sumerians already had plenty of deities of their own, including (the female) Inini, goddess of Venus. As the Semites intermingled with the Sumerians, their Ashtar gradually blended with Inini, to become for both peoples the goddess Ishtar—and we have already seen how *her* worship eventually spread through all the ancient world.

The two peoples swapped demons as well as gods, and the Semites learned from the Sumerian priests, for example, how to coax the demon of disease out of a person's body. This was done by plastering the sick person all over with a wet dough full of herbs and salt, saying the proper magic words and making the proper magic gestures all the while, then wiping off the dough— and with it, of course, the demon. The ceremony was called *kuppuru*. That word still survives in the Hebrew language, meaning "cleansing," and in the name of the Jews' highest holy day,

Yom Kippur, the "day of atonement," or of cleansing oneself of sin.

The Semites continued to increase in population in the Fertile Crescent until finally their Babylonian and Phoenician civilizations overwhelmed and absorbed that of Sumer. By this time, each city and smallest village had its own guardian god. These varied in characteristics and in names, but each was known familiarly by its worshippers as "the lord" (*el, bel, baal* or *beel*, according to the local dialect).

Meanwhile, one of the Semitic divisions—though it got along with all the other peoples of that area, and shared their gods and demons—had always considered itself a nation apart. These people were the ancestors of today's Jews, and they called themselves Israelites—"sons of Israel," the ancestor who had founded their dynasty. (*Israel* means "he who prevails with the god"—that is, with the *el.*) This nation was divided into thirteen tribes, each named after one of the sons or grandsons of that patriarch Israel —the Danites ("sons of Dan"), the Levites ("sons of Levi"), and so on.

After much wandering about the Fertile Crescent, the Israelites settled mainly in the land called "Canaan"—what is now Israel and southern Lebanon, but was then part of Phoenicia. There they acquired still another name. The Canaanites called these newcomers the Habiru, which can be translated as "the restless ones," and from which apparently derives the word Hebrew.

Twelve of the tribes of Israel were given land in Canaan, but the Levites were long denied any haven in the territory. Their forefather Levi had long ago murdered a prominent Canaanite, and all the descendant Levites were shunned as evil. So, as best we can piece their history together (because the folktales enshrined in the Old Testament are seldom historically accurate), the Levite tribe appears to have attached itself to the Hyksos—an Indo-European army—who were then marauding their way down the coast and into Egypt, which was by now the most advanced culture in the world.

The Hyksos did conquer mighty Egypt about 1700 B.C., and in gratitude to their fellow-traveling Levites, allotted them farmlands and pastures in the rich delta of the Nile—which the Jews named Goshen. But the Egyptians refused to stay conquered, and after a series of uprisings during the next 150 years, they succeeded finally in evicting the Hyksos invaders. Naturally, the Egyptians were not inclined to be too friendly to the Levites who remained in the country. So the Jews had their lands taken away, were made second-class citizens, and were generally despised and persecuted. Their lot worsened through the centuries until, 300 years later, the Levites were out-and-out slaves, building the great temples, monuments, and other works demanded by the vain pharaoh Rameses II.

Then along came Moses. According to tradition, the pharaoh decided to reduce the Jewish population, so he decreed that every male child born to the Israelite tribe should be put to death. When Moses was born (again according to tradition), his mother saved his life by letting him float downriver in a bulrush basket. Found and adopted by Rameses' daughter, Moses grew up and was educated at the royal court. We do not know the name of his real mother or father—in fact, we do not really know *his* name. *Moses* is merely a corruption of the Egyptian *meses* ("son of") and is only half a name. In actuality he would have been called "somebody-meses," as the pharaoh was called *RA*meses ("son of Ra the sun god.")

Moses had to become an outlaw when he killed an Egyptian whom he caught mistreating a Levite slave. Moses fled into the wilderness of Midian (somewhere in the neighborhood of today's Jordan) and the Midianites—nomad Arabs, therefore fellow Semites—took him in most cordially. He even married a Midianite girl and became the keeper of his father-in-law's flocks. Thus he did a good deal of wandering in the deserts and mountains between Midian and Egypt—and it was somewhere along there that Moses "found God."

The Egyptians among whom Moses had spent his youth—along with the Levites who were his true kinsmen—worshipped many gods. So did the Midianite Arabs among whom he lived more than half his life. Moses had spent most of his years as a herder in the wilderness, however, remote from communities of men and their organized religions. It is likely that he acknowledged as *his* chief god that violent one—most evident and most to be feared in his environment—who ruled over storm, thunder, lightning and the volcanoes which erupted at intervals in the mountain lands.

God first spoke to Moses from "a flame of fire out of the midst of a bush." In that volcanic country, this could have been a fumarole, a hole in the ground which spouts hot smoke or blazing gases. God made it plain that he was not just the "chief god" but that he was *the one and only God of the Israelites,* and was henceforth to be known as Yahweh. Furthermore, said Yahweh, his people were now simultaneously suffering in Egypt and mistakenly worshipping false gods. He had chosen Moses both to lead the Israelites out of that Egyptian bondage and to convert them to the worship of the Lord God Almighty.

Anyone being addressed by a burning bush is quite likely to accept what it says and to heed its commands. But, in any case, the concept of one and only one God may not have come as a surprise to Moses. Little more than a century before his time, pharaoh Ikhnaton had impressed upon Egypt the worship of a single, all-powerful god, the Aton. Though the religion of Aton had lasted for only twelve years, it is quite possible that isolated, stubborn sects of Aton worshippers had kept his memory alive. They would have been persecuted by other Egyptians, so the Atonists might well have fled to the desert and settled there to worship as they pleased. In his wanderings, Moses could have come upon one of these groups and listened favorably to their idea of One God.

When Yahweh commanded Moses to rescue his people from Egypt and lead them to the "land of milk and honey" which he promised they would find in Canaan, Moses protested that he had no power to persuade either the Israelites or the pharaoh that he was the appointed rescuer. So Yahweh endowed him with the ability to work some small miracles which ought to convince unbelievers. And Moses returned to Egypt, spoke to his people of the Lord awaiting them in the desert, then confronted the pharaoh—a new one by now, named Merneptah—and demanded the release of the Jews.

But the pharaoh "hardened his heart" and refused to let them go, whereupon Yahweh sent down a series of plagues on the Egyptians. Though each successive plague was worse than the one before, the afflictions failed to sway the pharaoh—until the last and most terrible plague of all. The Lord decided to kill the firstborn child in every house in the land, and gave Moses instructions to have every Israelite secretly mark the doorpost of his dwelling so the curse would pass over that house.

When all the Egyptians' firstborn children died, the pharaoh was not only ready to let the Israelites go but was eager to hurry them on their way. So, about the year 1230 B.C., the Israelites, taking time only to gather their flocks of goats and sheep, and to prepare "iron rations" for the journey, followed Moses out of Egypt. According to the Old Testament, Moses rescued from bondage *all* the existing Israelites in the world, to the number of 600,000 adult males, not counting women and children. But this figure is flatly impossible.

The Israelite nation may have numbered 600,000 souls in total—enough people to populate modern Boston, Massachusetts —but historical research has shown that the greater part of them had long before settled in Canaan and had never even seen Egypt. Also, the Old Testament gives a list of the oases at which the refugees stopped during their journey to the Promised Land. None of those watering holes could possibly have supported the encampment of such a horde. It is fairly certain that the only Israelites ever inhabiting Egypt, or enslaved there, or rescued from there, consisted of the one Levite tribe—and it may have numbered six *hundred.*

Moses led them across the Egyptian border through a "Sea of Reeds"—*not* the Red Sea, as the Bible tells us in a mistaken translation of the original Hebrew. When the pharaoh, for some reason, suddenly changed his mind about letting the Jews depart, and sent his army charging after them, it was not necessary for the "Red Sea" to part its waters for the refugees to get across. A sea of reeds would indicate a swamp, which the people on foot could slog through fairly easily, while it would have bogged down the heavy war chariots of the Egyptian army.

The pharaoh gave up, and the Levites were free and safe— except for the hazards of the long desert crossing they had to make. And long it was. According to the Old Testament, they took *forty years* to traverse the less than 600 miles from Egypt to Canaan. The Old Testament tells us that they did linger for intervals here and there, as at Mount Sinai (or Mount Horeb; the account is unclear), where Moses spent forty days and nights in converse with the Lord Yahweh, and is said to have brought down from the mountain the stone tablets inscribed with the Ten Commandments. Also, the refugees were delayed by frequent skirmishes with desert tribes of bandits. And they paused to parley with other, friendly, Semitic tribes, several of which joined their march.

Still, to account for forty years, we must assume that the Levites settled down to *live* for a time in some place or places—such as Sinai, for the Egyptians had copper mines there, and probably a mining town of some size. That town might also have been one of the sites of a sect still worshipping the Aton. Moses could have settled his followers there in order to indoctrinate them more firmly with the notion of accepting One God—theirs to be the Almighty Yahweh. We have at least one intriguing clue: the Old Testament's Psalm 104 is an almost line for line translation of the "Hymn to the Sun" written by Ikhnaton himself.

Regarding the Israelites' journey, the Book of Exodus is quite clear in telling how they followed as "the Lord went before them by day in a pillar of cloud . . . and by night in a pillar of fire." That is a perfect description of a volcano seen from afar. On the occasion of Moses' forty-day consultation with Yahweh, Exodus says of Mt. Sinai that "the smoke thereof ascended as the smoke of a furnace, and the whole mount quaked greatly." Again, an exact description of a volcano—which Mt. Sinai is not and never has been. The nearest volcanic activity was in Moses' former homeland of Midian, far to the northeast. So neither the Mt. Sinai of the copper mines nor the Mt. Sinai marked on our maps today, whether or not the same mountain, was ever the mountain from which the Ten Commandments are said to have been handed down.

It is doubtful that Moses himself ever had anything to do with the Commandments. Remember that he and his followers were, for most of those forty years, presumably wandering in the barren deserts. Then consider the Fourth Commandment—to work six days only, and to rest on the sabbath. This could well apply to a town dweller, but hardly to these nomads who had to tend flocks, to forage for pasture and water every day in the year. The Tenth Commandment—not to covet "thy neighbor's house . . . nor his ox, nor his ass," and so on—would apply to members of a settled community owning domesticated work animals, but not to a wandering people who had no houses or individual property at all.

We must bear in mind that the Old Testament was written long after the events it purports to describe, and deliberately tries to make Jewish beliefs and customs appear to date from the Jews' earliest history, when, in fact, most of them were developed slowly and over many centuries. Moses, as an old desert expert, probably did lay down the strict dietary commandments which Jews still obey—such as not eating pork, for the (original) reason that it spoiled very quickly in the torrid desert. But biblical scholars are fairly solidly agreed that the Ten Commandments were, like so much else in the Old Testament, composed by priests long after the time of Moses, when the Israelites had settled into their Promised Land.

Moses never got to set foot there, says the Book of Deuteronomy, because of a minor sin he had committed. Instead, Yahweh allowed him merely to glimpse that land of milk and honey from the top of a (still unlocated) Mount Nebo. Then Moses died there on Nebo and "no man knoweth of his sepulchre unto this day."

But the Levites—with the allies they had collected along the way: Zebulonites, Midianites and other Semitic tribes—swept down into Canaan. Their leader was Joshua, whose very name, meaning "Yahweh is salvation," indicates that the Levites were by then firmly dedicated to their one Lord God. Indeed, for centuries afterward, only men of the tribe of Levi were considered qualified to be priests of Yahweh.

As we know, that Promised Land was already inhabited by the Phoenician Canaanites and numerous settled tribes of Israelites, living together amicably. The Levites and their allies—hardened by their years in the desert—forced their way into this peaceful country and took over lands and towns without so much as a by-your-leave. The only inhabitants who fought back were the Philistines—Indo-Europeans who had crossed the Mediterranean from Crete and were now well established along the Canaan coast. It took centuries of battling the Philistines—and the Israelites were frequently conquered and subject to them—before these non-Semites were driven out of the country.

The Levites not only brought Yahweh as a new god for Canaan but they also brought some of the customs they had learned in Egypt. One of these was the rite of circumcision—the snipping-off of the foreskin from the penis of a boy baby. Heretofore, contrary to what the later written Book of Genesis tells us, only the Egyptians had practiced circumcision, to mark their men as "superior" to the men of lesser nations. Now the Levites, deeming themselves superior to non-worshippers of Yahweh, insisted that every Israelite be circumcised. (Many centuries later, when Judas Maccabeus defeated the anti-Semitic Greek and Syrian occupiers of Israel's province of Galilee, he forcibly circumcized all the surviving enemies to make them compulsory Jews.)

Every year since the Exodus, devout Jews have observed the seven-day celebration of Passover, in remembrance of the Lord's having passed over the Israelite houses while slaying the firstborn of Egypt. Since no one knew the exact date when that had happened, the Jews chose to celebrate Passover at the time they had been accustomed to celebrate the coming of spring in Egypt—that is, in March or April by our modern calendar.

Similarly, Yom Kippur, the high holy "day of atonement," was set in the Hebrew month of Tishri (our late September or early October), which is the first month of the Jewish New Year. This obviously dates also from the Levites' stay in Egypt, as that was likewise the Egyptians' New Year (because that was when the Nile River reached its annual high-water mark to irrigate all the surrounding farmlands), and the Egyptians also regarded the New Year as a time for "atoning for past misdeeds" and "turning over a new leaf."

Under King Saul and his successor, King David, all the Israelite tribes, their allies and the resident Canaanites were united into a single kingdom. The Philistines were driven away, and the country enjoyed a period of peace and prosperity. However, Yahweh had not yet become the one and only Lord God of the whole kingdom, because the renewed intermingling of cultures influenced the Jews to renew their recognition of the much older nature gods still worshipped by the Canaanites and other tribes. Even the Levites took rather laxly Yahweh's commandment that "thou shalt have no other gods *before me.*" In their view, so long as Yahweh was acknowledged supreme, there was no harm—and perhaps some benefit—in continuing to pay worship to the numerous gods of fertility, rain, harvest, flocks, and so on. Another circumstance was that Yahweh had declared himself to be the *God of the Israelites,* and they were his "chosen people." Thus the Israelites considered themselves a people divinely favored and superior to all others, and they jealously kept their God to themselves, making no missionary attempt to share him with others.

The theory that Yahweh was only for the Israelites so "localized" him that both the Israelites and other peoples came to believe that he would listen to no prayers uttered anywhere but on Israelite ground. To illustrate, a Syrian army captain named Naaman once came to be cured of leprosy by the Israelite prophet Elisha. Naaman, cured, was converted on the instant, and begged Elisha to give him two mule-loads of the soil of Israel to take back to Syria. He wanted to carpet a room of his house with that soil so his own thanks to Yahweh would be heard by Yahweh.

Under King Solomon—whom apparently not all his subjects considered "as wise as Solomon"—half the kingdom seceded and set up on its own. There was the northern Israel and the southern Judah (from which came the word *Jew*). Israel was mostly fertile, farming country. Judah was mostly grazing country for flocks and herds. These physical facts influenced their religious leanings. In Judah, Yahweh continued to reign, but in Israel the people relied more and more on the nature gods. Their fertility rites became orgies of blood sacrifices—even of their own infants— and of sordid sexual acts (to induce the gods to make their fields "bear abundantly"). Even those who still acknowledged Yahweh as chief god began to worship him by making offerings to images of bulls and serpents (both long-time symbols of fertility).

Now, Yahweh had always been—he said so himself—a "jealous" God, a "man of war," a God of "wrath," punishing men for the sins of their fathers "unto the third and fourth generation." After all, Yahweh had begun as a god of thundering storm and belching volcanoes. For years such prophets as Elijah and Elisha had preached against the wicked practices of those Jews who diluted their reverence for Yahweh by expending some of it on the worthless gods of other cultures. The prophets warned that Yahweh would not stand for this for long. And, sure enough, the lands of Judah and Israel began to be wracked with disasters. There were wars between the two kingdoms, wars with other Semitic peoples roundabout, and invasions by non-Semitic enemies from afar.

In 722 B.C., Israel was conquered by Assyria, and ten entire tribes of Israelites were marched at spearpoint off into oblivion. They are still referred to as the "lost tribes," and historians still speculate as to where they ended up—perhaps in India, Mexico, Japan, England, even (according to the Mormon Joseph Smith) in New York State. Then both Israel and Judah were conquered by the Babylonians. This time all the Jews were exiled from their homelands for seventy years, until Cyrus of Persia vanquished Babylon in turn and permitted the Jews to return home.

The Jews could only conclude that they had been punished for having neglected to pay the proper worship to Yahweh and *only* to Yahweh. As if this remorseful notion had not occurred to the people, there arose among them a number of fiery-eyed, thunder-tongued prophets to tell them so. Such men as Isaiah and Jeremiah preached sulphur-and-brimstone sermons threatening the Jews with further calamities if they didn't mend their ways and turn wholeheartedly to Yahweh.

But later prophets, such as Hosea, Joel and Zechariah, preached—for the first time—that the Lord God Yahweh should be worshipped not out of fear of his wrath, but because he truly loved his chosen people. Yahweh did not, said Hosea, demand sacrifices as did the old gods, but only faithfulness and right conduct. Joel predicted that, at a place called Har Megiddo, God would one day stage the greatest battle the world had ever seen —himself confronting all evil and defeating it forever, from which time the world would again be a Garden of Eden. (We speak of *Har Megiddo* now as "Armageddon," and use the word to refer to any completely catastrophic conflict. For instance, we fear that a nuclear war would be an "Armageddon.")

The prophet Zechariah foretold a glorious future for the Jews if they would remain steadfast in their worship of Yahweh and obey all his commandments. Zechariah, as had Isaiah before him, also prophesied the coming of a Messiah (king and deliverer) who would lead the Jews to greatness. Still another prophet, Jonah, was instructed by Yahweh in person to go and spread his religion among other peoples of the world. Jonah at first resisted —he wanted, like other Israelites, to keep Yahweh the private deity of the "chosen people"—but Yahweh chastised him, Jonah repented, and went forth to carry the word of God to the "Gentiles" (all non-Israelites).

From this point on, the Jews abandoned all other gods and acknowledged Yahweh as forevermore the one and only God. Further, they acknowledged that he was more than the God of the Jews, he was also the God of the whole universe and all beings. And now they began to elaborate considerably on their beliefs about and attitudes toward this Lord God Almighty.

They decided that his very name was too sacred to be spoken. If God is All, they reasoned, he should not be known by name, lest this imply the existence of other gods. They referred to him as *Adonai* ("Lord") and *Elohim* ("God," or, rather, the plural "gods," indicating that God contained and *was* all those other gods, or *el's*). Though the stricter Jews never pronounced the Sacred Name, they did, when they got around to compiling the Old Testament, set it down in writing (as YHWH or JHVH). Ages later, Greek, Latin and English translators of the Scriptures turned that into Jehovah.

The Jews also supplied Yahweh with a host of attendants, known to us as angels. These seem to have been at least partly adopted from the friendly Persians who had delivered the Jews from their captivity in Babylon, for those angels known as cherubim and seraphim are very like some of the deities of Persia. Originally, they were not angelically beautiful humanlike beings, wearing glowing gowns and shining wings. The Jews first visualized the cherubim as winged bulls and the seraphim as fire-breathing serpents. Still later, Christianity adopted the Jewish God complete with all his angels, and added to them, until there were nine "orders" attendant on God: seraphim (the highest), cherubim, thrones, dominions, virtues, powers, principalities, archangels and angels.

As in so many other cases, the gods of the old religions became the demons of the new Judaism. Those old-time gods variously called *el, bel, baal* and *beel* were lumped by the Jews into one devilish Baal—and the Jews condemned all the other societies which still worshipped and sacrificed to this conglomerate devil. The Jews called all those old (hence evil) practices *bosheth* ("shame") and incorporated that word (and scorn) into the new names they gave to old gods and rituals. Their one-time goddess Ashtarte they now abhorred as Ashtoreth, a demoness. You'll note that the name change was effected merely by substituting the vowel sounds of *bosheth*.

The Jews had, for ages, sacrificed their own children to a being called Melech—meaning simply "king" and referring to whichever was the ruling god (including Yahweh in his turn). Now they referred to that god, again substituting the vowels of "shame," as "the Molech"—and shuddered. The Jews did not change the name of the hill (Tophet) where they had once burned their children as sacrifices, nor of that ravine (Sheol) where they had unceremoniously dumped the charred little corpses, but they now gave both names the same meaning—what most of us call "Hell."

The Jews no longer had a fierce and demanding God, but a loving and giving one. Yahweh no longer threatened and punished; instead he dispensed mercy and justice. He no longer insisted that his worshippers cringe and grovel before him, but encouraged them to stand upright and walk beside him as companions. He made blood sacrifice an abomination, and asked only loyalty and obedience.

The Jews were the first people to find a religion which lifted them from a primitive moral level toward a high ideal of ethics. They were not the first to conceive of a single Lord God, but they were the first to conceive an enduring one, who endures to this day. The Jews now were certain that their Yahweh was the Creator and benevolent caretaker of the entire universe—and they freely spread the word of him, so that the whole world could discover and enjoy the benefits of this one Lord God Almighty.

But there was one impediment. Others already had independently conceived their own Lord God Almighty.

THE
MYSTERIOUS
EAST

When I have presented one corner of a subject to anyone, and he cannot learn the other three from it, I do not repeat my lesson.

— CONFUCIUS

Until about fifty years ago, it was believed that the Indian sub-continent had never harbored anything but primitive tribes until the first traces of civilization were brought by those ever-wandering Indo-Europeans. In the 1920's, however, archaeologists began to dig up evidence, in the region which is now Pakistan, that there had existed an oasis of native culture as long ago as 3000 B.C., or about the same time the civilization of Sumer was beginning to flourish in the Fertile Crescent. We know little about this early Indian civilization, except that it occupied a 400-mile-long portion of the Indus River Valley, with a tremendous and handsomely laid out city at each end. These cities contained palaces, citadels, drainage and sewage systems, paved streets, and elegant public baths. All the lands outside that "Shangri-La" valley, including what is now India proper, were peopled with nothing but savage tribes of the jungle and desert.

How the "Indus Valley Civilization" came into being is a mystery. It seems to have sprung up almost full-blown and lasted for some 1,500 years, making it one of the longest-lived civilizations the world has ever known. It had a diversity of population, ranging from Negritos (midget blacks) to tall, light-skinned peoples. Even when the cities were new, these Indus Valley inhabitants were well advanced in agriculture, the arts, architecture, and commerce, engaging in trade with Sumer, nearly 2,000 miles away.

Their religion was based entirely on the stars, which, they believed, revolved around a central supreme god, and it was here that astrology was first invented. The study of the movements of the stars at least made the Indus Valleyites master mathematicians—hence skilled architects, adept businessmen, and so on—which may have been the only good that ever came out of the "science" of astrology.

It is for certain that astrology did its inventors little good. These Indus Valley people obviously lived—numbly and unquestioningly—according to "what the stars foretold." Some scholars have called them "a civilization of sleepwalkers" because, while they built a respectable culture, it never progressed beyond its original level. During all their fifteen centuries, they neither advanced nor changed one whit. Evidently on the stars' advice the society remained static and fatalistic. So, when the Indo-Europeans descended into the valley, about 1500 B.C., they took over the land and the cities without resistance from the natives.

Besides astrology, only one vestige of this civilization survived, and that is its god around whom the whole universe revolved. No one knows what he was originally called, but he is now the malevolent god Siva of Hinduism, the major religion of modern India. (Pakistan, where the Indus Valley Civilization and the god Siva were born, today is of the Muslim religion.)

India's Hinduism is unique among the major religions in that it had no single founder or prophet, but just gradually "grew" over thousands of years—and in innumerable different directions. There is no central church of Hindusim, no formalized organization, and no governing council. Its gods are all nature gods, good or evil. Siva became the first of the evil gods when he was borrowed from those ancient star-worshippers. Other Hindu gods—

Varuna (the sky god), Agni (fire), Indra (war and storm), Vayu (wind), and so on—were borrowed from the Indo-Europeans.

The basic trinity of Hindu gods—if such a fragmented and splintered religion can be said to have any basics—are Brahma, Vishnu and Siva. Brahma was the Creator of the universe, who, having created it, then sat back and has ever after remained too remote even for worshipping. The universe has been kept in balance since its creation by the opposing forces of Vishnu the Preserver, Siva the Destroyer, and their respective mates. Vishnu's wife Lakshmi is the goddess of good fortune; Siva's wife Kali is the black goddess of death.

Vishnu is believed to have visited the earth frequently in human guise. Once he came as Krishna, who later starred in what must be the longest poem ever written, the 120,000-line *Mahabharata*. In this interminable epic, Krishna first appears as a sort of Panlike youth, forever skipping about, playing a flute, and flirting with farm girls. As a man, he becomes the great warrior-hero of one of India's perennial civil wars. Vishnu and his human incarnation Krishna have become the focus of many offshoot Hindu cults which revere one or the other aspect of this god above all other deities.

Some Hindus prefer to worship evil: the death-goddess Kali still has her devotees. For 700 years, she was adored by a cult called the Thags (hence our word "thug"), professional stranglers and robbers who regarded their occupation as a religious duty they owed to Kali—their profits being only incidental. There is no knowing how many people (probably millions) the Thags killed "to the greater glory of Kali." But, in the 1830s, when the British finally stamped out the cult, a man named Buhram, who had been the Thag leader for forty years, bragged that he alone had strangled 931 persons to death.

Other Hindu sects and cults have numberless other and different beliefs, and variously recognize one or another of the gods as the top-ranking one. Some sects reserve their highest reverence for certain animals, trees, stones or even *diseases*. The various groups worship in many different ways—sacrificing goats, sheep or buffalo by cutting off their heads before an image of the favored god (or, if this is too expensive, substituting a coconut or pumpkin "head"), by chanting mystic charms and drawing mystic diagrams (so mystic that they are meaningless even to the worshippers), by bathing in the sacred (but filth polluted and putrid) Ganges River, and so on. The listing of varieties of Hindu belief could be extended indefinitely, so varied are their religious practices and so heterodox are their beliefs.

About the only aspects of the Hindu religion on which all Hindus agree are (1) a belief in reincarnation (being born again after death) and (2) the caste system, the vilest idea still pervading any major religion, and one which has hampered India's progress throughout her long history.

Caste means "social level," and in India there are four main levels: the Brahmans (highest), the Kshatriyas, the Vaisyas, and the Sudras. Within each of these, there is a "pecking order" of countless subdivisions. Of the lowly Sudras the lowest of the low are the *pariahs*, literally "the untouchables." Even their shadow falling on someone of higher caste is considered repulsive. By the rules of Hinduism, a person is born into his or her caste, and fixed there all life long—no matter how intelligent or gifted he or she may be. Caste determines what occupation a person is allowed to pursue, where he may live, even who his friends may be. (He will not associate with anyone of lower caste, and cannot associate with anyone of higher caste.)

This system was set up about 1,800 years ago by the Brahmans, the priests of early Hinduism—who, as one would expect, made themselves and their descendants the topmost caste—and the system has persisted ever since, in spite of all would-be reformers and the passage of numerous "equal rights" laws. To this day, a lower-caste Hindu's only hope of elevating his status lies in that other major belief: reincarnation. But there are rules about that, too.

A person who behaves badly in this life, according to Hinduism, will be reborn in a lower caste or even as a lesser animal. A person who lives righteously can hope to be reborn into a higher caste. If he goes on, life after life, climbing upward on that moral ladder and accumulating a good *karma* (the sum total of his conduct in all his lives), he will eventually reach *nirvana* (that is, be absorbed into the "universal soul") and be freed from the endless cycle of death and rebirth. This is the highest aspiration of the devout Hindu, and, as you might expect, many "shortcuts to nirvana" have been invented.

One of these is the practice of Yoga, which promises to hurry one toward that communion with the universal soul by means of spiritual and physical exercise. Depending on who is teaching it, Yoga may involve any or all of these elements: bodily contortions, simple meditation, self-hypnotism (concentrating on one's navel or the tip of one's nose), chanting over and over some "mystic" phrase, curious exercises like "breathing in through one nostril and out through the other," or contemplating mind-boggling riddles like "What is the sound of one hand clapping?"

No yogi (a practitioner of Yoga) has ever been known to disappear instantly into the universal soul of nirvana. Nor has any yogi ever proved that he could do such things (claimed for Yoga) as float in the air, nor has any yogi ever demonstrated superhuman mental powers or knowledge. But there is no doubt that the *gurus* (masters of Yoga) have attained extraordinary physical endurance. They can go without food, drink, or even breathing, for periods that would mean sure death for an untrained person. However, no yogi has ever explained exactly what the purposes of these accomplishments may be, or why they should interest the universal soul.

Many of Hinduism's beliefs about reincarnation, nirvana, and so on, were adapted from the later religion of Buddhism, which began to be preached in India about 2,475 years ago. This was founded by Siddhartha Gautama, born a prince of the Kshatriyas, direct descendants of the Indo-Europeans. Young Gautama was brought up in royal surroundings, carefully sheltered from the harsh facts of life in India. However, at the age of twenty-nine, he took a ride through the countryside—for once unattended—and saw four sights that changed his life: an aged man, a sick man, a dead man, and a poor but serene beggar-monk. To Prince Siddhartha, these symbolized the fates to which man must come. Three of them were sad and only one desirable: a life of poverty with freedom and contentment.

Whereupon Gautama slipped away from his palace—abandoning wife, child and throne—and himself became a wandering beggar. He sought not to do good deeds, but to think good thoughts, in order to purge his soul of impurities. He went without food and mistreated his body so that his soul would invite the notice of Brahma, the supposedly unattainable Creator. (In other words, like so many other holy men and shamans, Gautama sought to achieve a mental state conducive to visions.)

Once he starved himself for forty-nine days and nights, sitting under an old bo (fig) tree. At the end of that time, Brahma finally revealed himself to his devoted servant. Thereafter, Gautama no longer traveled alone, but was followed by admiring beggar-students, who gave him the name Buddha ("the enlightened one"). To these followers, Buddha taught what Brahma had taught him; namely, that a man's sorrow, suffering and dissatisfaction could be abolished by his following a "middle path" of moderation in all things.

The path was (and is) eightfold: (1) *right belief*, (2) *right resolve*: to renounce pleasure and to harm no living creature—a true Buddhist will never so much as step on an ant, swat a mosquito, pluck a flower, or even drink a glass of water in the dark, for fear of swallowing and destroying some unseen water bug or whatever—(3) *right speech*, (4) *right conduct*, (5) *right occupation*, (6) *right effort*: to keep free from evil and devoted to good, (7) *right contemplation*, and (8) *right meditation*, to the point of virtual self-hypnosis. The end result, said Buddha, would be nirvana, which he defined as a complete and blissful detachment from all things worldly, a "waking up" to the joys of union with the Creator.

Though Buddhism is currently the religion of nearly 200 million people around the world, it has scarcely a handful of believers in its native India. This was mainly the doing of the Brahman caste of Hindus, who feared that Buddha's democratic teachings would break down the rigid caste system. So they merely incorporated into Hinduism some of the less "revolutionary" principles of Buddhism, and convinced the Indians that Buddha was *not* a unique prophet of a new religion, but merely another human guise in which the Hindus' own Vishnu had again visited earth.

While Buddhism was gradually being abandoned in India, however, it was being eagerly received in the surrounding countries which we know today as Burma, Nepal, Sri Lanka, Thailand, Cambodia, Laos and Vietnam. It made converts in Tibet who carried it into China, whence it spread into Korea and Japan. Along the way, Buddhism, like most evangelistic (convert-seeking) religions, underwent some changes, elaborations and "improvements."

For instance, it split into *two* Buddhisms, the Hinayana ("lesser vehicle") and the Mahayana ("greater vehicle"). The Hinayana is closer to the original teaching of Buddha, still maintaining that the much-desired nirvana is only a "waking up" to spiritual bliss. The Mahayana preaches that good Buddhists will avoid an afterlife of torment (or Hell) and will enjoy perpetual delight (or Heaven).

In Tibet, Buddhism was much debased by being merged with the Tibetans' age-old religion called Bon—demon-worship of such beings as the dragon-headed Sridevi and the yak-headed Yamantaka. Together, Bon and Buddhism became Lamaism, or "the monks' religion." Chances are that things have changed since Tibet came under the iron rule of Communist China in 1959. But, at least until then, one of every six male Tibetans was a monk living in a lamasery and having no other occupation. The highest-ranking monk, the Dalai Lama, ruled both the country and its religion. He served for life and when he died the country was scoured for a baby boy born at the exact moment of the high lama's death who resembled that lama, having similar moles, birthmarks, whatever—and that child, were he ever so humbly born, would be appointed the next Dalai Lama.

Tibet's prime national industry—the obsession of every Tibetan—was religion. All the nation's arts, architecture and handicrafts were influenced by Lamaism. Everywhere, on rocks and walls, banners and streamers, was inscribed the "mystic" prayer, *Om mani padme hum*, or roughly, "Hey! Jewel in the Lotus. Hum!" When a Tibetan was too busy to repeat that over and over, he achieved the same effect by twirling a prayer wheel inscribed with the incantation. But nobody, including the lamas, has ever been able to say exactly to what deity that prayer is addressed, or even exactly what it *means*.

It is only human nature that we see something of the mysterious and therefore important in anything hidden, whether it is out of sight or simply beyond our understanding. Just so, "the wisdom of Tibet" has become proverbial. Surrounded by the world's highest mountains, Tibet was for ages almost unreachable by foreigners, and the Tibetans didn't welcome foreigners, anyway. It wasn't until 1904 that there began to be any considerable traffic into Tibet from the outside world. And those foreigners who did get in not only found the Tibetans fanatic about their religion but also found the religion, with its puzzlers like *Om mani padme hum,* impossible to understand.

When looked at from the "mystic" point of view, it seems obvious that the long-hidden Tibetans simply *must* be possessed of long-hidden and profound wisdom, along with secrets unknown to us ordinary humans. Hence a great many people—especially those beguiled by the occult and the supernatural—still believe that the Tibetans know (but won't reveal) how to achieve eternal life, perpetual world peace, heaven on earth, communication with flying saucers, and the like. Looked at from

another point of view, however, the Tibetans are merely a primitive mountain people, isolated from modern knowledge, holding fast to a nonsensical mumbo-jumbo which in turn holds them fast in ignorance. (We could as well expect to find mystic wisdom among the gibbering, snake-fondling faith cults in certain backward areas of the United States.)

Fortunately for Buddhism, it has not elsewhere degenerated into such abracadabra. China and Japan especially embraced one of the offshoot Buddhist sects, originally called *dhyana* ("contemplation") in India. That name became *ch'an* in China and *zen* in Japan. This form of Buddhism is closely allied to the Hindus' Yoga, in that it stresses deep meditation in the cross-legged position (*zazen* in Japanese) and concentration on unsolvable riddles or nonsensical conundrums (*koan*) like Yoga's "What is the sound of one hand clapping?" This is intended to shock one's mind out of its everyday groove of rational thinking and into a state of *satori*, or nonintellectual, instinctive, deep-down enlightenment.

Though Zen Buddhism has lost its early popularity in Japan, and now lags far behind Christianity and Shinto (Japan's homegrown belief in nature gods), Zen has in the past quarter-century won many converts in the United States. It became particularly popular among those who were disillusioned with America's materialistic (success-oriented) religions and so turned to the obscure and mystic wisdoms of the east.

One might wonder why Buddha deserves a place in a book about gods, since he never preached a "religion" but only a "way of life," and—except for urging a "union with the creator"—never mentioned gods at all. (Indeed, even devout believers in other religions can in good conscience practice Buddhism at the same time.) The fact is that Buddha gradually became an object of worship himself. No Buddhist actually calls him a god, but hundreds of thousands of images of him, and temples built in his honor, now stand everywhere in the Oriental countries—and Buddhists address him with reverence, thank offerings and prayers.

Buddha would have loathed the idea of his being thus elevated to godhood. But he'd have got an ironic laugh out of it, too, because all those statues were carved by Orientals, and they "made their god in their own image." Practically everybody everywhere, conditioned by the appearance of those images, thinks of Buddha as having been a fat, heavy-lidded, sleepy-eyed, complacent-looking Oriental. In fact, as a direct descendant of the Indo-Europeans, Siddhartha Gautama would have resembled a modern-day Iranian—tall, energetic, olive-skinned, with dark, wavy hair and wide-open, sparkling brown eyes.

Buddhism had to contend (and combine) with demon worship in Tibet. In Japan, it had to overcome (and did, for a while) the well-entrenched Shinto. In China, however, Buddhism became just one more in a welter of religions, gods, philosophies, superstitions, and ways of life.

Among Chinese religious practices, the foremost is that of ancestor-worship, already mentioned. The Chinese conceived of Heaven as a world situated directly beneath China and identical in every detail of geography, climate, economy, government, and so on. On dying, a good man or woman went there and went on living just as he or she had on earth. As late as 1910, one Chinese would lend money to another with the agreement that it would be repaid in the next world. And, as we have seen, that belief in an afterlife was the reason for burying with a dead person all the goods he or she would need there.

The dead might also benefit by the meritorious doings of living descendants. Suppose a man performed some great service for China, and the ruler elevated him to the nobility. The royal decree would make that title retroactive for five generations, so that the man's ancestors, back as far as his great-great-grandfathers and -mothers, would also be entitled to live in the luxury of nobles down there in that underground after-China.

The underground world also contained a very efficient Hell, where persons who had behaved badly on earth were subjected to various sorts of torture. The worst of these tortures—and the one most dreaded by the ancestor-worshipping, family-obsessed people—was for the dead sinner to be condemned to stand before a sort of magic TV set and watch the results of his evil deeds as they affected his descendants on earth. For generations he would have to stand there, see his children and friends suffering because of his sins, the family fortunes diminish, finally the ruin and extinction of his whole family line—while he could only watch, unable to intervene to help them or to turn his eyes away from the awful sight.

The Chinese also by this time believed in a multitude of nature gods and demons. In event of drought, famine, earthquake or other disaster, they made human sacrifices to these beings. For example, when that "dragonlike" Yangtze river flooded, it was the practice of riverside villages to tie one of their choicest young maidens to the best bed available and shove it out into the current—hoping that this "bride" would placate and divert the river demon.

In the face of a calamity which threatened the whole country, the khan or emperor himself would pray that the sins of the people should be heaped on his head, and then, to atone for those sins, he would sacrifice his own head. Well, not exactly *his* head; the Chinese rulers have always been a most practical class. The emperor, once he had assumed his "burden of sin," would cut off a lock of his hair, paste it on the forehead of a black bull—and the *bull* would be beheaded.

China as a whole never abandoned all its gods, demons and superstitions. But a few great thinkers did devise more rational "ways of life," and the more literate and intelligent Chinese turned to these philosophies as their guides to good behavior.

The earliest of China's renowned sages was Lao Tzu, born about 600 B.C. Lao Tzu, in the teachings that he called *Tao* ("the way"), emphasized that a man should bend his efforts toward an acceptance of the great powers of the universe rather than fuss about human relationships and everyday doings. Tao's main tenet was that everything in the universe contained opposing forces—the *yin* and the *yang* (good and evil, male and female, light and dark, all the opposites there are)—which, if not tampered with, would forever keep everything in balance. Taoism, to put it simplistically, taught: "Let well enough alone. Enjoy, don't analyze." For example, don't take a clock apart to see what makes it tick, because, even if you manage to put it back together and it still works, most likely it will never again work as well as it did before.

About fifty years later was born K'ung Tzu, better known today as "Confucius." Though he often visited the aged master Lao Tzu, and respected his teachings, Confucius developed a philosophy of his own that was quite the reverse of Lao Tzu's teachings. He believed in ignoring the supernatural and concentrating on human relations. For example, he gave China the Golden Rule for living—"Do unto others as you would have others do unto you"—nearly six centuries before Jesus Christ and his Apostles made it a maxim for the Western world. (Confucius, however, phrased it slightly differently: "What you do not want done to yourself, do not do to others.")

Anyway, both Lao Tzu and Confucius thought in terms of giving all men—whether they governed their lives by staying attuned to the Higher Powers or by trying to get along better with their fellow men—a richer life on this side of the grave. And neither of the sages embellished his philosophy with religious overtones; neither claimed to have had visions or revelations from on high; neither of them even went about preaching and seeking converts. Instead, they taught by example: living good lives themselves and inspiring others to do likewise.

Since both Lao Tzu and Confucius were pure philosophers, they would hardly merit inclusion in a book about gods—except for what happened long after their death. The followers of Lao Tzu decided that for best results in living in tune with the universe, they needed experts to instruct them in the finer points of yin and yang. Thus there sprang up Taoist shamans and fortune-tellers of all sorts, all claiming to possess the only true knowledge of such forces. Meanwhile, the followers of Confucius turned his teachings of "good manners" into stiff rules of etiquette, his "compassion" into bored tolerance, and his "goodness" into a mask which they wore only in public, while privately they took every possible advantage of their fellows. Later, both Taoism and Confucianism eagerly seized on the principles of Buddhism when it reached China about A.D. 200, and incorporated many of its teachings into their own.

Eventually, neither Taoism nor Confucianism bore any resemblance to the teachings of the masters. And the only thing they had in common with each other was that both had turned their founders into gods. The self-appointed priests and shamans of the two "ways of life" elaborated them into "religions," complete with formalized rituals, offerings, and godlike devotion to be paid to Lao Tzu and to Confucius, who had never been—and never wanted to be—anything more than good and upstanding, moral but mortal men.

Chinese religion remains a hodgepodge to this day. The Chinese living in the Free World maintain a bewildering variety of beliefs, some managing to juggle all the beliefs simultaneously. (In Communist China a belief in anything but Chairman Mao Tse-tung is rigorously discouraged.) A most amusing, but quite truthful, description of Chinese religion nowadays is given by Dennis Bloodworth, a long-time resident of the Orient, in his fascinating book *The Chinese Looking Glass*.

According to Bloodworth, the modern-day Chinese religion "is the one stew in the world that has everything in it, *including* the kitchen stove. A Chinese, it seems, will worship Confucius, Buddha, the Goddess of Mercy, the Kitchen God of the Stove, the Jade Emperor, the Mother of the Western Heaven, the Queen of the Sea, his own grandfather, the Eight Immortals, a piece of red paper inscribed with the name of a man who once lent him twenty dollars at a difficult moment, the Monkey God, the Big Dipper, and the man who killed a tiger in the street of his home village and subsequently emigrated to the United States, where he appears to be doing very well.

"They say there is a rabbit pounding out the pill for the Elixir of Life in the moon, together with the woman who first filched it from her husband. This man was a general who was given it as a reward for shooting down nine of the ten suns that once surrounded the earth, this leaving only one. And the first thing I knew of an eclipse in Singapore, in 1960, was a tremendous rattling and banging of gasoline cans set up by all the people in a nearby Chinese kampong. They were shooing off the Sky Dog to stop him eating the moon, which is, of course, made of cake."

ZOROASTER,

MOHAMMED,

AND

THE BAB

Allah obliges no man to more than he has given him ability to perform.

– THE QU'RAN

The three major religions of the western world, Christianity, Islam and Judaism, claim nearly one and a half billion believers among them, almost half the earth's population. Another religion —with a minuscule membership—only some 130,000 people still adhere to it—is regarded as insignificant and outmoded even by those who know that it is still in existence. Nevertheless, that now-dwindled religion, Zoroastrianism, was once a mighty force in the world. And, in a sense, every Christian, Muslim and Jew (though probably without recognizing it) still believes in some aspect of Zoroastrianism.

The man we call Zoroaster (from the Greek rendition of his name) was born Zarathustra, son of a camel rancher, in the northwest corner of Persia, about 628 B.C., at a time when Persians worshipped or feared a couple of hundred different nature gods and demons. While yet a youth, Zoroaster was skeptical about these superstitions, and when he left home at the age of twenty, it wasn't to seek his fortune but to seek answers to his religious questions.

One absurd tradition has it that he spent the next ten years living in the desert and subsisting on camel cheese; another tale has it that during those years he lived in a cave without speaking a word. In reality he seems to have done a good deal of talking— that is, asking people questions about their gods and demons, but never receiving a reply that satisfied him.

Then, at the age of thirty, he got an answer that would have satisfied or at least silenced the most skeptical of men. Zoroaster was seated on a riverbank when suddenly there materialized before him a figure nine times larger than a man. Introducing itself as Vohu Manah ("Good Thought"), this being picked up Zoroaster and carried him skyward, into the presence of Ahura Mazda ("Sovereign Knowledge"), the Supreme Being and Creator of the World.

This great God was surrounded by six attendants: Vohu Manah, who had brought Zoroaster, Asha Vahista ("Highest Righteousness"), Khshathra Vairya ("Divine Kingdom"), Spenta Armaiti ("Pious Devotion"), Haurvatat ("Salvation") and Ameretat ("Immortality"). Zoroaster was awed, bewildered and perhaps frightened in the midst of this august company, but not so much that he failed to notice one detail—he saw that in the combined radiance emanating from all these beings about him, he cast no shadow.

Ahura Mazda himself instructed Zoroaster in the true religion he had sought for so long, its doctrines and its duties, and sent him back to earth to be its prophet. During the next several years, when Zoroaster wasn't trying to preach this new religion, he was being visited by one after another of Ahura Mazda's six attendants, each of whom gave him more details of what would eventually be called Zoroastrianism.

In essence, the religion recognized Ahura Mazda as the God of Light, in both senses of that word: the lighting up of men's minds and the light that abolishes darkness (this had been impressed on Zoroaster by the loss of his shadow in the presence of his God). People of other religions have often mistakenly called the Zoroastrians "fire-worshippers." It is true that every Zoroastrian shrine kept an "eternal fire" burning, but not as an object of worship; it merely symbolized the Light actually worshipped. Three other concepts of Zoroastrianism are the ones which, as mentioned, still remain in the beliefs of Christianity, Islam and Judaism.

First, Ahura Mazda was surrounded by a number of attendants who acted as his messengers to earth. Judaism borrowed this idea, to provide a "heavenly court" for its Yahweh, and also called these beings "messengers" (*malakhim*). Both Christianity and Islam later adopted the idea from the Jews, and provided God and Allah with their "heavenly hosts." (Our word "angels" is from a Greek translation of *malakhim*.)

Second, Ahura Mazda had an opposite number, or adversary, in the being known as Ahriman, who led a legion of *daevas* ("demons") in trying to work mischief in the world and thwart all the good doings of Ahura Mazda and his worshippers. Some Zoroastrians, in fact, believed that Ahura Mazda and Ahriman were born twin sons of some "cosmic mother," who assigned the one to do good and the other to do evil. At any rate, Judaism and later Christianity took this concept, only making the adversary (Satan) not an equal of God but a former underling who had rebelled and fallen from grace. Mohammed took the idea in turn from the Jews when he founded the religion of Islam in which Allah's adversary is known as Shaitin.

Third, according to Zoroaster, a person's soul went either to the "House of Song" or the "House of the Lie" after his death, depending on his behavior during his lifetime. Immediately upon his death, a person would find himself walking across the "Bridge of the Separator." If he had been a wicked person, that bridge would be so narrow that he could not keep his footing, and he would plunge into the foul, filthy, torment-filled "House of the Lie." But a good man would find the bridge wide and easy to cross into the eternal bliss of the "House of Song."

Of course many another religion had much earlier entertained this same notion of reward or punishment after death. Zoroaster himself may have borrowed it from as far back as ancient Egypt. But it was from Zoroastrianism that Judaism, then Christianity, and then Islam borrowed their Heavens and Hells.

("Paradise" comes from a Persian word for a walled garden or park, *pairi-daeza*.) The oldest of these religions, Judaism, had originally conceived of an afterlife that was nothing but dreary for all men and women, whether good or wicked: a sort of gray mist in which every soul wandered alone and forlorn throughout eternity.

We maintain yet one more leftover from Zoroastrianism. That religion's early priests were called Magi, and they were popularly supposed to have power over demons, over the forces of nature, and so on. So they gave us the enduring word *magic*.

In its first years, Zoroastrianism was just about as scorned and insignificant as it is today. Despite his fervent preaching, it took Zoroaster ten years to win his first convert—and that was his own cousin. But then he found two helpers—a rather odd couple, a king and a horse. In his wanderings, Zoroaster had come to what is now the Khurasan region of Iran, then the domain of a King Vishtaspa. This king had a favorite black horse which unfortunately was dying, and none of the Persian shamans, called Karpans, could cure it. Zoroaster did cure it, however, by performing a minor miracle. Thenceforth he was King Vishtaspa's closest friend and confidant, and he soon won the king over to the worship of Ahura Mazda.

From then on, Zoroastrianism was on the march. It became the state religion of Vishtaspa's whole kingdom, then of the entire Persian Empire. The old gods and demons were discarded (or made into minor deities and trifling evil spirits of the new religion). The Karpans, who had used their bogus sorceries to become tyrannical and demanding priests, were banished in favor of the kindlier Magi. When Zoroaster died, in 551 B.C. (he himself was by now almost a god to his followers), he had founded a religion whose temples sprouted from Armenia in the west to the borders of India in the east.

Zoroastrianism then held sway for 200 years—during which time Judaism borrowed those aforementioned beliefs—until 330 B.C., when Alexander the Great conquered Persia. Alexander imposed his Greek gods on everyone he defeated. Zoroastrianism persevered, however, as an "underground" religion, and had a rebirth 500 years later, about A.D. 226. It had changed considerably since Zoroaster's time. Whoever was ruler of Persia (and the

crown changed heads frequently) claimed to rule by the divine power of Ahura Mazda. The new priests were as tyrannical as the old Karpans had been.

It happened, also, that Zoroastrianism revived just as Christianity was making its first great headway as a new religion. So the two faiths competed fiercely for converts throughout the Middle East, and, as a result of this rivalry Christians and Zoroastrians became bitter enemies. But the enmity did not prevent the Christian Fathers from "fighting fire with fire" by borrowing whatever Zoroastrian beliefs they thought would appeal to their prospective converts.

Christianity was to encounter rougher competition from other religions elsewhere, but it did go on growing, while Zoroastrianism did not. The religion of Zoroaster was dealt its death blow in A.D. 651 when the Muslim Arabs overran Persia and killed its King Yazdegerd III. The conquering Muslims did not prohibit the old religion—indeed, like the Jews and Christians, they appropriated some of its beliefs—but almost all the Zoroastrians became Muslims for purely selfish reasons of self-advancement under the new rulers.

Today there are no more than 10,000 Zoroastrians in Persia

(now Iran) and about 120,000 Zoroastrian Parsees living in the area of Bombay, India. The year of 1975, in which I am writing, is, to those few remaining faithful Zoroastrians, the year 1343, for they date their calendar from the coronation of Yazdegerd III in 632, the beginning of the reign of that last king "on whom shone the Royal Glory of Ahura Mazda."

Coincidentally, 632 was also the year in which died Mohammed, prophet and founder of the world's second most popular religion, the Nation of Islam. Today, the various sects and denominations of Christianity total nearly a billion members; Islam counts about half that many, but it is still growing. Like Zoroastrianism, Islam was the creation of one man, and, like Zoroastrianism, it had a hard time getting started. For the first two-thirds of his life, Mohammed was a shepherd, a soldier and finally a quite prosperous merchant and civil judge in the Arabian city of Mecca. At the age of forty, however, he retired to a cave outside the city and, after a period of meditation, emerged to announce that he had had a revelation from God to spend the rest of his life as God's "sixth and final prophet."

It should be explained that until Mohammed appeared, the Arabs were nothing like the comparatively united people they are today. The divisions among the numerous Arab sheikdoms and tribes were mainly caused by the multitude of different religions they practiced. Some had embraced Judaism, some Christianity, some Zoroastrianism, but the greater number of tribes each worshipped some set of pagan gods. For instance, the Sabaeans of what is now Yemen had more than one hundred deities, headed by a holy trinity composed of Sams (the sun goddess), Warah (the moon god), and Attar (the god of Venus; male, but note the name's resemblance to Ishtar, Astarte, *et al.*). The Sabaeans were nomads, who lived by herding goats, sheep and camels, but once a year, in the month they called Du Mahajjat, they all converged in a pilgrimage to their main temple at the town of Ma'rib.

Mohammed's "new" religion of Islam was actually assembled from those principles he found most worthwhile in Judaism, Christianity, Zoroastrianism and from several of the pagan Arab religions. Mohammed recognized the same Lord God Almighty as the Jews and Christians, though he never gave God a personal name like Yahweh or Jehovah. God, to Mohammed and his followers, was simply *al Ilah* ("the God"), and note the linguistic similarity of *Ilah* to the Jews' *El* and *Elohim*—and *al Ilah* was eventually condensed to *Allah*.

The name of Mohammed's religion, *Islam*, means "submission" (to the will of Allah), and a member of Islam is a *Muslim*, meaning "one who surrenders" (to the will of Allah). The religion, its founder, and its followers have been called many names by other peoples. Mohammed's name has been variously rendered as Muhammad and Mahomet; the religion has been known as Mohammedanism, Mahometanism, and so on. The Muslims themselves have been variously called Moslems or Mohammedans; in olden times they were called Mussulmans and—especially by the Christian Crusaders—"the infidels" and "the paynims" (or pagans). In retaliation, the Muslims call all non-Muslims, "the unbelievers."

When Mohammed came out of the cave, he announced to his fellow citizens of Mecca that God had in the past sent five prophets to spread his "holy word" on earth—Adam, Noah, Abraham, Moses and Jesus. Each of them had given the world various fragments of "the truth," but now he, Mohammed, had been assigned to have the last word, so to speak, and bind up all the other prophets' teachings into a perfect whole.

At first, the Meccans simply derided Mohammed. (You can imagine the reaction if your grocer or hardware dealer suddenly announced to your hometown that he was the latest prophet in such a distinguished line-up.) When Mohammed stubbornly continued to preach, the Meccans became downright angry. You see, Mecca was an important market center at the intersection of several major trade routes of the time, and with merchants continually on the roads coming from and going to Syria, Iraq, India and Egypt. To accommodate these myriad merchants of different nationalities and religions, Mecca had a sort of all-purpose temple called the Kaaba, a little building containing images of the deities of every religion that had then been heard of. It even included a statue of the Virgin Mary holding the Child Jesus. Now here was Mohammed, a former businessman himself, about to antagonize all those visiting traders by condemning their religions and demanding replacement by a totally new one. The visitors would surely take their rich caravans elsewhere, and Mecca's prosperity would be ruined. After making numerous attempts to reason with Mohammed, the citizens decided to shut him up permanently by assassinating him. Mohammed soon got wind of this plot, however, and fled from the city.

Mohammed's *hijrah* ("flight") from Mecca in the year 622 has enshrined that date in the Islamic calendar as the year 1. What made the "hegira" (as we call it in English) so important was that Mohammed ended up in the city of Yathrib. The citizens there had heard of his new religion, and approved of it. They welcomed Mohammed with open arms—a whole city of instant converts. Indeed, they made him dictator of Yathrib. It was later even renamed in his honor, Medina, "the City" (that is, "of the Prophet").

With a solid headquarters and a cityful of new Muslims to send abroad to carry his message, Mohammed soon began making converts all over Arabia, including even money-minded Mecca. In fact, Islam was self-propagating. All the separate tribes and sheikdoms of Arabia had long recognized that their only hope of power and prosperity lay in becoming a united people. As more and more people in all parts of the country turned to the new religion, others realized that Islam was the uniting force they had long needed—and they joined, too.

It is said that Islam's main appeal to the Arabs was Mohammed's early pronouncement that any Muslim who died "fighting for the faith" would go immediately to a Heaven full of lovely women, luxurious surroundings, elegant foods and other earthly delights. That may well have been one reason, but another was Islam's extreme simplicity, as compared with its competing religions. The Muslim must observe only five religious practices:

1. At least once in his life he must recite aloud (and understand what he is saying, and mean it) the Islamic creed: "There is no god but Allah; Mohammed is the prophet of Allah."

2. Five times a day he must prostrate himself in the direction of the prophet's birthplace, Mecca, and say a prayer. (Originally, in the hope of converting all the Jews of the Middle East to

Islam, Mohammed bade his Muslims face toward Jerusalem to pray. But the Jews remained firm in their Judaism, so Islam did an about-face toward Mecca.)

3. The Muslim must go without food through all the daylight hours of every day of the holy month of Ramadan.

4. The Muslim must give alms to any needy fellow Muslim.

5. If it is not absolutely impossible, every Muslim must at least once in his life make the *hajj* ("pilgrimage") to Mecca. This idea of the *hajj* (and the name of the month, Dhu-l-hijja, recommended for the trip) Mohammed may have adopted from those pagan Sabaeans mentioned earlier. Wherever he got it, it has proved to be the strongest force uniting all of Islam's diverse peoples. The pilgrims who rub elbows at Mecca may include white Albanian mountain men, brown Javanese islanders, blacks from Senegal, swarthy Moors from Morocco, even American Negroes. All those who make the pilgrimage go home with a renewed faith in the worldwide unity of Islam—and with pride in the title they are now allowed to add to their name: *Hajji.*

Certainly Mecca long ago forgave Mohammed for the upheaval he caused; the city has prospered far more from Muslim pilgrims than it ever did from those earlier caravans of mixed religions. The Muslims' destination is the original Kaaba, still a little stone cube of a building but now stripped of all its one-time idols and images, and enclosed within the walls of the Great Mosque of Mecca. There the hajji kisses "the black stone which fell from heaven." (It really did; it's a meteorite.) Muslim tradition has it that the stone was dropped by Allah to mark the birthplace of his prophet. Actually, it fell and was ensconced in the Kaaba, and was worshipped for itself alone by pagan Arabs, ages before Mohammed was born. Ages before the Meccans began to fill the little building with the images of the traveling merchants' gods.

There are a number of "thou shalt not's" in Islam, either borrowed from other religions or banning things Mohammed found abhorrent in other religions. A Muslim must follow many of the same dietary restrictions—never eating pig meat, for instance—as those laid down for the Jews. In addition, he is forbidden to drink wine, because Mohammed once saw one of his closest disciples dead drunk, and was disgusted. (This has led later Muslims to argue heatedly as to whether they can drink alcoholic beverages "softer" or "harder" than wine, such as beer and whiskey.) No Muslim mosque can have bells or music, because these were part of the Christian worship rituals that Mohammed despised. No Muslim mosque can contain images or pictures of human or animal figures, because they are reminiscent of the pagan idols Mohammed swept out of the Kaaba. (Thus the Great Mosque of Damascus has one entire wall decorated with a mosaic picture of a lovely city, but there is not a human or so much as a camel on its streets.)

One of Mohammed's prohibitions rather amusingly illuminates the human side of the prophet. It seems that once, when he was still a merchant, Mohammed was given a tongue-lashing by a customer, a little old lady. Years later, when he was setting down the writings which now comprise the *Qu'ran*, the Muslims' holy book, Mohammed spitefully specified that no "old woman" would ever be admitted into the Islamic Heaven, as she would be sure to disturb the peace of the place. He eventually mellowed and relented, and struck out that passage. But it gave rise to arguments that are still going on among various sects of Islam, as to whether or not women have souls at all.

By the time Mohammed died, in 632, Arabia was for the first time in history a single nation with a single religion. And Mohammed was regarded as more than a prophet, more like a god himself, accorded by Muslims the same reverence that Christians pay to Jesus Christ. In later centuries, his religion spread as far east as Malaysia and as far west as Spain, carried there by the Moors who occupied Spain from 711 to 1492. (When the Spaniards finally expelled the Moors, they also abolished Islamic worship, but there remain many traces of Arabic culture in the Spanish languages, arts and architecture, carried over even into Spain's former colonies in the Americas.)

To this day, Islam continues to collect converts, and to play a part in the politics of even non-Muslim countries. In 1947, Muslim Pakistan seceded from its union with Hindu India simply because of their peoples' religious differences. The newly independent "emerging" countries of Africa and elsewhere—Christian missions have for centuries been trying to convert them—are more inclined to turn to Islam because they associate Christianity with the domination of the former imperialist rule of England, France, Spain, and other European countries. Even in the United States, thousands of blacks have disavowed Christianity because it was the religion of the old-time slave owners and have formed their own Nation of Islam, better known to unbelievers as the Black Muslims.

One offshoot of Islam could prove to be the religion to end all religions, simply because it wants to *include* all of them. This religion began in 1844, when a young Muslim named Mirza Ali Muhammad announced in Shiraz, Persia, that he was henceforth to be known as Bab ed-Din ("Gate of Faith") and persuaded some of his fellow Muslims to join him in "improving" Islam. The Bab, as he was familiarly known, wanted to throw out some of the pages of the *Qu'ran* and substitute passages from the holy books of other religions.

The Bab didn't get very far with this, as the Muslim-controlled government of Persia soon imprisoned him as a troublemaker. His followers, known as Babis, tried all sorts of threats and demonstrations to get him released. When, in 1848, they publicly declared that Babism was seceding completely from Islam and setting off on its own as a new religion, the government did let the Bab out of prison, but only to execute the "unbeliever." In turn, the Babis tried to assassinate the Shah of Persia, which resulted in thirty of them being rounded up and put to a horrible death.

From then on, Babism led a harried existence. One Babi after another assumed the title of the Bab, while he had to keep moving his headquarters—from Baghdad in Persia to Constantinople in Turkey to Acre in Syria—as one Muslim government after another expelled these "agitators." The last leader of Babism, Mirza Hussein Nuri, made sweeping changes in the homeless and formless religion, including taking for himself the new title of Baha Ullah ("Splendor of God").

The Baha'is, as the members now called themselves, made a determined effort to gain respectability for their religion, and even—for the first time—set down its principles and guidelines. They were still vague on some points; for instance, Baha'ism has yet to decide whether there is a Heaven and Hell, or even any afterlife at all. Baha Ullah died in 1892, but his son Abbas Effendi (called Abdul Baha, "Servant of Splendor") even more energetically promoted the religion. He gained converts in Persia, sent missionaries to Europe and himself visited England and America. In the United States there are now some 8,000 Baha'i converts who, though the current Secretary of their Spiritual Assembly is an American, still refer to the late Abdul Baha as "The Master."

Baha'ism teaches that there is only one God, who has manifested himself in all religions (the major ones, anyway), and that therefore all these religions are "true," differing only on minor points that can eventually be compromised. The Baha'is believe that God sent a number of prophets to earth, among them Abraham, Moses, Christ, Mohammed and, of course, the Bab and Baha Ullah. Baha'ism hopes some day to unite all religions, to create a one-world government and an international language. Until that happy day, the Baha'is emphasize simplicity of living, the doing of useful labor, and the giving of service to suffering fellow men.

THE GODS

AND THE

CHRISTIAN

GOD

We are all supposed to believe in the same thing in different ways.
It is like eating out of the same dish with different colored spoons.
And we beat each other with the spoons, like children.

— ESMÉ AMARINTH

Christianity, at its beginning, brought no new god into the world. Its founder, Jesus, was a Jew and, like all devout Jews, he believed in Yahweh, the one Lord God Almighty. However, Jesus himself was by definition a demigod: born of the union of a mortal woman and the Lord God (or his spiritual aspect, the Holy Ghost). According to the New Testament's Book of Matthew, both Yahweh and Jesus informed the Apostles that Jesus was genuinely the son of God, though born to the newlyweds Joseph and Mary. Jesus told the Apostle Peter that he was in fact the Christ ("the anointed one"), the Messiah whose coming had been foretold by the Jewish prophets of centuries before.

Isaiah, for one, had written in 742 B.C.: "Behold, a virgin shall conceive, and bear a son, and shall call his name Immanuel [God with us]" and that this son would lead the Jews to their era of greatest glory. Jesus convinced many of his fellow Jews that he was that Immanuel, the Messiah, the Redeemer—and those who believed were the first Christians. The majority of Jews, however, denied Jesus' claim that he was to be their Messiah. They waited, and are still waiting, for the birth of the real Immanuel.

This is a book about gods. If we accept the prevailing Christian beliefs, Jesus' career as a demigod could be sketched in a very few lines and this would be a very short chapter. All we know of Jesus' life and teachings is what a lawyer would call "hearsay," the reminiscences of some of his disciples in their books of the New Testament. But even the book generally accepted as the earliest written—that of St. Mark—was not set down until sometime between 30 and 40 years after Jesus' death. Much can be forgotten—or exaggerated—even by a saint, in 30 or 40 years. And if we add up everything that all those disciples wrote about Jesus, we find we have a record of just about 50 *days* in his whole lifetime of 33 to 36 years.

Nevertheless, a discussion of Christianity belongs in a book about gods, if only because one of its most interesting aspects—which helped to make it the foremost of all of today's major religions—is the use the early Christians made of the other gods

existing at that time, even while denouncing, discarding and displacing them. Indeed, the few details we have of Jesus' life and doings are obscured by what may have been simple coincidence —or, again, may have been the Christians' deliberate borrowings from other gods and other religions.

For example, many another god and demigod was believed to have been, like Jesus, miraculously born of a virgin. Mithras, the most popular god of the early Persians, and who later became popular from India to Rome, was said to have been born of a virgin. He was also born at the winter solstice, the shortest day of the year, which, by the Roman calendar, fell on December 25.

It may seem irreverent even to speculate that perhaps Mary was not a virgin in the modern sense of the word (never mated), or that Jesus was not miraculously born. But many a sage theologian has suggested that "virgin birth" is a misreading of the original accounts. The books of the New Testament were first written in the common language of the Middle East at that time, a sort of corrupt Greek called *koiné*. The term used for Mary in that language, *parthenos*, was later translated to the Latin *virgo* and finally to the English *virgin*. But those older words never meant a woman absolutely untouched by a male—such a maiden would have been called *virgo intacta* in Latin, for instance. The words *parthenos* and *virgo* meant no more than an as-yet-unmarried woman.

However, whether Mary was acclaimed "the Blessed Virgin" by mistake or not, later Christian churchmen were happy to accept her as such, and to certify Jesus as having been sired by no mortal father like Joseph, but by the Holy Ghost. This put him on an equal footing with all the other virgin-born gods—Mithras, Dionysus and others—with whom Christianity was competing for converts. It also made Mary the nearest thing to a goddess in the Christian religion. Thus, when Christian missionaries attempted to convert some nation or tribe which worshipped pagan gods, the missionaries could offer them God and Jesus instead; when they encountered those whose chief deity was a goddess, they could try turning the people's worship to Mary.

It must be said that the very earliest Christian missionaries did not *offer* or compromise at all; they *insisted* on others accepting their religion. Jesus—and Christianity—was born in Palestine (what was once Israel and Judah) when it was just one colony in the "worldwide" Roman Empire. Some early Christians traveled to the Imperial City of Rome, and from there helped to diffuse Christianity throughout the whole Empire. But, while they did make converts, they also made themselves highly unpopular with other Romans.

Rome, because it had conquered and absorbed so many other nations of so many different religions, had long maintained a tolerant attitude of "live and let live." In fact, Rome allowed the construction, throughout the Empire and even in Rome itself, of innumerable little temples, shrines, synagogues and altars dedicated to the worship of innumerable gods, goddesses and even demons. No one objected, therefore, when one more religion—Christianity, then regarded as just another Jewish sect—began its preaching in Rome.

At least, no one objected *at first*. But it soon became obvious that the Christians, unlike their Roman hosts, did not believe in letting everyone worship according to his choice. They publicly and loudly declared that their God, and only their God, was the true Creator and Ruler of the universe; that all other gods were false, and their worshippers were deluded in this world and doomed to Hell in the next. This seemed unfair to the other religions of the Empire, so the Roman officials tried to discourage such inflammatory speeches, but the Christians persisted. They refused to recognize or tolerate any other gods, including the Roman Emperor, who claimed to be one. They refused to serve when they (like other Roman citizens) were called to the army in time of war, on the ground that the legionnaires worshipped Mithras.

Such attitudes naturally made the Christians disliked by the majority of Romans, and soon they were the victims of persecution. It delighted the public when the Emperor put on a spectacular entertainment in the Colosseum by "throwing Christians to the lions." This may not have delighted the Christians, but they went to their deaths without complaint, believing—as did the Muslims some centuries later (who may have got the idea from those Christian martyrs)—that "to die for one's faith" meant immediate transition from this cruel world to a delightful Heaven.

Nevertheless, as the old saying has it, "You can catch more flies with honey than with vinegar." The Christians' attitude toward others gradually changed from "be a Christian or be damned" to one of conciliation and adaptation of those non-Christian beliefs. In short, the missionaries began to tailor Christianity to the taste of whatever particular people they were trying to convert.

For example, the New Testament says nothing about the month and day of Jesus' birth, and the earliest Christians didn't celebrate it. However, those Christians of the east—in Palestine, Egypt, Abyssinia, etc.—somehow came to pick January 6 as his birthday and made a holy feast day of it. But now the Christian missionaries in Rome stopped demanding conversion and began the new tactic of wooing converts to Christianity. In Rome, Mithras' birthday was such a popular holiday that it gave the Christians an idea. They appointed December 25 to be Jesus' birthday as well, and pleaded with their prospective converts "not to celebrate this solemn day, like the heathen, on account of the *sun*, but on account of him who *made* the sun."

By the year 300, all the scattered groups of Christians had settled on December 25 as "Christmas," and had made the former birthday of January 6 the date of "the Epiphany" instead. (That is, the day when the infant Jesus was first seen by the Three Wise Men and his divinity was recognized.) Actually, so far as scholars can estimate, Jesus was probably born in the late autumn. Nobody can fix the *year* he was born in, because the early Christian calendar-makers inaccurately set the Year of Our Lord 1 some four to seven years after his birth, meaning that the Christ was born some time between 7 and 4 B.C. ("before Christ").

Nowadays, in some countries the "Christmas holidays"—with continuous church services, festivities, bonfires, and so on—cover the whole span from December 25 to January 6 (or "Twelfth Night"). In other countries—Mexico, for one—Christmas is a day for quiet holy worship, and January 6 ("The Day of the Three Kings") is the day for gift giving and merriment. In still other countries—most notably the United States—the "Christmas season," meaning the gift-buying season, starts a month or more before Christmas, with such familiar heralds of the holy day as recorded carols blaring from be-tinseled shopping centers.

Christmas edged in and displaced the Midwinter Day celebrations of several other peoples besides the Romans. And Christianity turned the holy days of still other gods and beliefs to its own advantage. Another date important to many nature worshippers was the spring equinox, and Christianity didn't have to invent an arbitrary holiday to supplant that pagan celebration. The Jews' Passover, as we have seen, was originally adapted from the coming-of-spring festivities in Egypt. And we know that Jesus was crucified during the season of Passover.

It was the Roman governor's custom to gratify his Jewish subjects by pardoning some condemned criminal at the time of Passover. This time, a murderer named Barabbas and the "traitorous conspirator" Jesus were scheduled to die, and the governor, Pontius Pilate, offered to free Jesus. But the Judaic priests, who were the cause of the accusation of Jesus as a political plotter, now lashed the mass of Jews into a rage against him. The crowd outside Pilate's palace demanded that he release the criminal Barabbas instead. So Jesus went to the cross, and died, and three days later, according to a goodly number of his Apostles and other followers, Jesus arose from the tomb.

The Christian missionaries did not have to adapt this miracle to other peoples' beliefs, for many already believed that the season of spring was brought about by some god or goddess arising from a temporary death or from an imprisonment in the underworld. The Greeks believed that Adonis brought the spring when he came up from his wintry stay in Hell with Persephone, to spend the sunny half of the year with Aphrodite. The Phrygians believed the spring came with the annual visit of their god Attis, the Assyrians had their spring god Tammuz, and the Anglo-Saxons their spring goddess Eostre.

Some zealous and not very knowledgeable Christian priests denounced these other beliefs as "devilish counterfeits" and "offensive parodies" invented by other religions to mock and debase the miracle of Jesus' resurrection from the dead. But of course all those other springtime rebirths dated from ages before Christianity. Wiser Christian priests seeking converts among those pagans simply let them go on with their coming-of-spring celebration, but gradually made it "in honor of Jesus" instead of the original local god.

Curiously, in English and other languages of the Teutonic family, that holy season is still called Easter (German *Ostern*, etc.) after the pagan goddess Eostre. In languages of the Latin family, the holy day bears a name like *pâques* (French), *pascua* (Italian and Spanish), and so on. These are adaptations of the Hebrew word *pesach* ("Passover"). Throughout Christendom, the day of Jesus' greatest miracle, the day that proved his divinity, is given a name from another religion.

Midsummer Day, celebrated in so many sun-worshipping pagan societies, was likewise appropriated by the Christians and is still celebrated, though now as the birthday of Jesus' cousin and instructor, John the Baptist. The Muslims, who (like the Christians) supposedly shun all pagan practices, also (again like the Christians) still celebrate Midsummer Day just as their ancestors did. Now called *l'ansara*, the holiday is even more an oddity in Islam than in Christianity, because the Muslim calendar is geared to the moon, not to the sun or the seasons. Since this gives the Muslim year thirteen months, all the Muslim holy days slide gradually around the circle of the solar year—all but *l'ansara*, Midsummer Day by any other name.

In Rome, August 15 was the day of a feast sacred to the goddess Diana, the Huntress. Christianity converted it into a day honoring the Assumption (bodily ascension) of the Virgin Mary into Heaven. From the Celts of Ireland, the Christians took two pagan holidays—March 17 and November 1—and turned them into more "truly religious" days. March 17 was the date set for the start of spring, and a day when the Irish went quite wild. Christianity tamed them (and the celebration) somewhat by making it the feast day of St. Patrick, the first Christian missionary to Ireland.

November 1 had long been New Year's Day for the Celts, from Ireland through Wales and Scotland to northern France, because it represented a breathing spell between the end of harvesting and the beginning of winter. On that day, shamans told people's fortunes for the coming year, so the day was presumed vaguely "magical" and eerie: the dying of the old year, dead human souls mooning about, and the like. The Christians turned November 1 into a catch-all celebration, calling it All Saints' Day or Allhallowmas. The night before, Allhallow's Evening, got its name eventually condensed to Halloween—and the supposed spooks and real pranks of that night are leftovers from the ancient Celts' pagan beliefs and antics.

Christianity has adapted to its own use more things than just the holy days of other religions. It has become a tradition, though not dictated by Christian doctrine, to lighten the solemnities of Easter with the frisky Easter bunny and its Easter eggs. These are borrowings from the oldest and most primitive people who celebrated—often with shameless orgies—the "fertility" of springtime. The egg is an obvious symbol of impending birth, and the rabbit—with its rapid-fire capacity to produce young—has always been a symbol of fertility.

From the pagan tree-worshippers of Britain and northern Europe, Christianity borrowed the Christmas tree, sacred to its original devotees because it was evergreen (fir, pine or other conifer) and did not "die" every winter. The Christmas tree certainly never had anything to do with Christ or his birthday, as such trees are unknown in the land where he was born.

In many countries, Christian missionaries have taken over the sacred places—hills, springs, groves of trees—where the pagans were accustomed to worship their original gods, and there have built Christian churches. If there was already a crude building—or even, as in Mexico, a magnificent temple or pyramid—they would tear it down and often use its stones to build their new church. The native people, so long used to worshipping at that holy spot, would still congregate there, and would gradually find themselves worshipping the God of the Christians.

Another Christian-adopted leftover from older religions is the "scapegoat"—a creature or figure regularly burdened with a people's sins and then banished or destroyed. Until four centuries ago, in the devoutly Christian villages of the Bavarian Alps it was the custom, every Midsummer Day, to parade a scarecrow through the streets and then burn it to ashes. The effigy was then known as the *Lotter* ("rascal"), and its burning got rid of any sinful rascality among the villagers. However, in the 1500's, the priest Martin Luther sparked the Reformation which split Christianity into Roman Catholic and Protestant churches. Luther, of course, was hated and reviled by those who remained faithful to *The* Church (that is, Catholicism). So, in those Catholic alpine villages, it was easy to change the scarecrow's name from Lotter to Luther, and annually burn *him* instead.

One aspect of Christianity strikes a faint reminder of an even older and more primitive—even savage—religious ritual. Jesus said, on the occasion when he miraculously shared five loaves of bread among the thousands gathered to hear him, "He that eateth my flesh, and drinketh my blood, dwelleth in me, and I in him." Jesus' act of symbolically sharing himself among all his followers is still retained in the rite of Communion practiced by Roman Catholic and most Protestant sects, when every communicant gets a bit of bread and, in some denominations, a sip of wine or grape juice, thereby reinforcing himself with the goodness and moral strength of his Lord Jesus. This idea of a worshipper being spiritually nourished by "eating his god" would (and does) horrify those of some other religions. But an African or Polynesian cannibal would have found it quite natural and praiseworthy.

Another long-time practice of primitive peoples was the worship of idols, supposedly embodying nature gods and demons. Yahweh's Second Commandment to the Israelites was, "Thou shalt not make unto thee any graven image. . . . Thou shalt not bow down thyself to them, nor serve them. . . ." And the Commandments were accepted by the Christians as binding on them, too.

But the Christians also adopted Judaism's "angels of the Lord"—and increased their number. Then the Christians added another holy order—that of the saints, once mortal men and women who are now presumed to hold a high rank in Heaven, because of their extremely holy life here on earth or their suffering an untimely death for the sake of their religion, or their working of miracles. The official recognition of sainthood is known as "canonization." Most Christian denominations still believe in angels—Gabriel will blow the trumpet signal for Judgment Day, for instance—but since the beginnings of Protestantism, only the Catholics have continued the practice of canonizing.

On the façade of the Church of England's cathedral at Coventry looms a giant-sized "graven image," glorious wings outspread, of the archangel Michael. And in every Roman Catholic church will be found "graven images" of many saints, all as expensively gold-leafed and costumed as the church can afford. The Catholic fathers maintain, however, that these are not idols, but merely reminders of the holy men and women represented, and are intended only to inspire churchgoers to live lives as holy as theirs were.

In any Catholic church, one can find worshippers praying—sometimes to the image of the crucified Jesus, but also to the image of the Virgin Mary, or to that of some other favorite saint. Praying to images violates Christian doctrine, especially as expressed in the Second Commandment, and such devotees have in effect reverted to the paganlike recognition of a multitude of deities. Of that multitude, they direct their prayers to the deity-saint they feel most kinship with or whose help they need most urgently. (St. Jude is supposed to "make possible the impossible," St. Anthony of Padua is believed to help people find lost objects, and so on.) Flowers and little gifts and coins are left at the feet of these statues. In really superstitious communities, particularly in countries where Catholicism is the only major religion, you will find the robes of a saint's image studded with pinned-on things like tiny tin legs or cutout advertisements for kitchen appliances. These are either tokens to remind the saint of what some worshipper has prayed for—the cure of a rheumatic leg or the acquisition of a new refrigerator perhaps—or they are thank-you notes for the saint's having provided same.

Many a nation, city and village has its own special patron saint, who may be the recipient of more prayers and devotion than either God or Jesus. The Mexican town in which I live is named for St. Michael, and his feast day (September 29) is a fiesta—church services, bell ringing, music, feasting, fireworks—far more impressive than any other celebration of the year, including Easter and Christmas.

But the Virgin Mary, foremost of all saints, is the patroness of more places than any other. All over the Christian world, you will find towns, churches, shrines, chapels with names like Our Lady of (say) Midville, or Santa María de Midville, or The Virgin of Midville. New York's Kennedy Airport has three sanctuaries, one for each of the "major" faiths, where travelers can say a prayer; the Catholic sanctuary is called The Chapel of Our Lady of the Skies. These countless different Mary's (depending on the country, her image may be of white, black, yellow or other complexion) are recognized or tolerated by the Catholic Church as "aspects" or "emanations" of the One Blessed Virgin. But the townsfolk of Midville, who revere their particular Our Lady of Midville, regard her as a real and separate and special Virgin Mary giving undivided interest to *their* welfare.

While liberally borrowing gods, devils, beliefs and customs from other religions and from pagans, there is one instance in which Christianity has made a determined effort to divorce itself from another faith. That one is its own "parent" religion, Judaism. Though a Jew was the founder of Christianity; though Christians worship the same God as do the Jews, and scorn the same Devil; and though the Jews have never shown any resentment or reluctance about sharing these concepts, the Christians gradually came to disown their connection with Judaism and tried to sever themselves from their "Jewish roots." For example, for nearly 300 years, Christianity's most solemn holy day, Easter, commemorating Christ's rising from the tomb, was observed during the week of the Jewish Passover. After all, that *was* the time of year when Jesus had been crucified and resurrected. But in 325, at their Nicene Council, the Christian elders decided to disassociate Easter from Passover so far as possible. So now the western Christian churches—those of the East have differing customs—observe Easter as the first Sunday after the full moon following the spring equinox, which means it can fall on any Sunday between March 22 and April 25. The first Friday after that full moon is Good Friday, marking Jesus' crucifixion.

This complicated way of fixing Easter's date results in yearly changes of other church observances—since the date of Easter determines the forty preceding days of Lenten austerity, plus Ash Wednesday, Palm Sunday, Trinity Sunday, the feast of Corpus

Christi, and other holy days which date either forward or backward from Easter. The system is too cumbersome for the average lay worshipper to work out for himself, so he must depend on a church calendar marked with these "red letter days."

Too, the system frequently does not work out quite as its innovators intended. Every so often, when that post-equinox full moon appears on a Sunday, Christians actually commemorate Easter, and Christ's return from the dead, *before* the day on which he died. Also, the Nicene Council's attempt to put a gap between Easter and Passover was rather unsuccessful on other counts. Since the Jews use a calendar partially attuned to the moon, all their holy days, like those of the Muslims, drift around the circle of the year. Thus, four years out of every five—despite the maneuvering of the Nicene Council—Easter does fall within the week of Passover. Other attempts to cut Christianity loose from Judaism have been no more than superficial—such as requiring Christian men to take off their hats in church simply because Jewish men keep their hats on in the synagogue.

Reference to these and other fussy rulings is intended only to illustrate how the simple truths laid down by Jesus gradually got buried under layer after layer of organization, elaboration, interpretation, explanation—and the formalization of rituals, ceremonial attire, priesthoods, sainthoods, church architecture, and so on.

Practically everything that Jesus demanded of his followers in the way of behavior can be summed up in his saying, "Thou shalt love the Lord thy God with all thy heart, and with all thy soul, and with all thy mind. This is the first and great commandment. And the second is like unto it, Thou shalt love thy neighbor as thyself."

It was not until the ninth century that Jesus was acknowledged a god himself—or at least a manifestation of God. In the New Testament, which was begun a generation after his death, Jesus was already repeatedly referred to as Our Lord. A bit later, Christians recognized Jesus as sufficiently godlike at least to be their go-between with the real God, and so prayed directly to Jesus. The ninth-century councils of presbyters made it official— God is actually a Holy Trinity of three-in-one: God the Father (remote in Heaven), God the Son (Jesus, who was God temporarily made flesh for the purpose of communicating with man), and the Holy Ghost (a spirit emanating from, and identical with, both the Father and Jesus), which spirit inhabits every devout, sincere Christian.

As we have seen, in its very earliest days Christianity had to fight for existence—and Christians had to die for their beliefs. Most of them did it nobly, in the belief that "our blood is the seed of the Church." In later days, Christianity was sometimes its own worst enemy. At times, Christian popes and rulers waged wars to *conquer* converts to their religion. This was naturally resented by the prospective converts, and by peace-loving Christians as well. At other times, the Church used the torture chamber and the burning stake to threaten Christians who deviated in the slightest from its strict doctrines. At still other times, the Church decided that "reasoning" posed a threat to the unquestioning faith it demanded, hence forbade Christians to read any but "approved" books.

Yet, all the time—when Christianity was being threatened from outside or feeling threatened from inside its own ranks, and even when it split asunder into Roman Catholicism and Protestantism—it was evolving into the major religion which made the frankest appeal to man's intellect rather than to his emotions or traditions. For example, Christianity more than any other religion has given the greatest impetus to both the fine arts and the lively arts—painting, poetry, music, statuary, drama, architecture and literature.

Though the Church took a rigid stand in the Middle Ages—"He who is not with me is against me"—Christianity later relaxed its stance to make a more universal appeal. Like the earliest Christians, who did not hesitate to gather converts by adapting elements from their former religions, the modern Christian Church, both Roman Catholic and Protestant, has learned to move with the times and bend to the changing ways of mankind. Unlike many other religions, Christianity does not look always to its past, nor pride itself that it has not changed a particle since its beginning. (It does not, for example, demand adherence to outmoded dietary laws.)

Instead, Christianity stands ready to consider any idea that appeals to the human spiritual need—whether it comes from other religions, philosophies or the behavioral sciences. It stands willing to absorb whatever ideas it finds helpful, and to reject those it finds harmful (for instance, remnants of superstition and other such leftovers from barbarism). In short, Christianity tries to blend into its God worship all that is best of man's spiritual beliefs. It can be said of a person who lives by Christian teachings today—whatever religion he claims to profess, or even if he claims none at all—that he or she is "a true Christian."

GOD

AND THE

GODS

TODAY

There must be something as infinitely superior to human personality as human personality is superior to a grain of sand.

— ABRAHAM WOLF

ITEM. Scientists have identified nearly two billion different animal species on this earth—mammals, fish, birds, insects, and so on. Of all those billions of species, only *seven* are known to wage organized warfare against their own kind: five sorts of ants, one type of termite . . . and man.

ITEM. If we date organized religion just from the birth of Judaism, the oldest faith still existing, in those 5,735 years there have been recorded about 15,500 wars, for an average of nearly three wars every year somewhere in the world.

ITEM. In that same span of time, say legal historians, an estimated 35 million civil laws have been passed in an unending attempt to legislate human behavior, yet every year more and more criminals commit more and worse crimes.

ITEM. From past centuries to recent times, men have—for the greater glory of one belief or another—waged bloody holy wars, sent Crusaders against the "infidels," slaughtered countless innocents in witless witch hunts, burned the irreplaceable libraries of "heathen" peoples like the Aztecs and Maya, tortured and slain innumerable "heretics" and "unbelievers."

ITEM. Right now, the people of India and Pakistan—people of identical race and lineage—wage sporadic wars against each other, simply because India is Hindu and Pakistan is Muslim. Right now, the Jews and Arabs—people of the same Semitic family—wage almost continuous war because they chose divergent religions. Right now, in Northern Ireland, people of identical nationality, even worshipping the same God of the same Christian religion, wage a brother-against-brother civil war, because one side is Roman Catholic Christian and the other Protestant Christian.

Considering this record, many cynics have sneered, and even pious men have pondered sadly, "What good is God, or any number of gods, if the world goes on being afflicted with evil, misery and misbehavior?"

Well, perhaps one reply to that is the answer a doctor gave to a dissatisfied patient. The patient had come to report that he was feeling rundown and sickly; the doctor examined him and gave him a prescription; the patient returned some time later, said he was still feeling poorly and complained that the medicine hadn't been worth its price. "Oh, no?" said the doctor. "Just think how much worse you'd be feeling if you hadn't taken it!"

Until about two hundred years ago, God and religion were more powerful, immediate and highly regarded forces in the lives of most people than they have been since. People depended on their God or gods—if not to make the world a Garden of Eden—at least to give them comfort and solace when things went wrong. But toward the middle of the eighteenth century, with the coming of the Industrial Revolution and its avalanche of new inventions, man began to boast of his own superior powers, and God began to be neglected.

For millions of years, man had traveled and transported his goods at no more than ten miles an hour, the speed of a good horse. Now the steam locomotive whisked him about at four times that speed. The telegraph enabled him to communicate

instantly with other men at distances immeasurably farther than he could shout. And so on and on, as the inventions proliferated. The airplane took him, for the first time, entirely off the face of the earth. The radio brought him information and entertainment "out of thin air."

Man himself was working wonders that no God or gods had ever accomplished. All of a sudden, in a sense, science was the new religion, and scientists were the new deities. Priests, ministers and rabbis insisted that any scientist's genius was a gift of God, and that all these wondrous inventions worked in accordance with God's laws of nature. But such preachings often went unheard in the public's clamor of admiration for their new toys, tools and weapons. These were things that could be seen, touched, used—material benefits, as opposed to the immaterial, God-bestowed benefits of goodness, mercy, justice and the like (not to mention such concepts as Heaven and Hell, neither of which could be proved to exist).

Then, after World War II, men began to be disillusioned with science. The scientists had provided—with their nuclear weapons and intercontinental missiles—a far more immediate doom than Hell. They had given man the means of destroying himself, his entire species and his whole world, in one great, instantaneous holocaust. Man's faith in the benevolence of science gave way to fear of Armageddon. But this still did not mean that men and women flocked back to the comforting arms of religion.

Since the beginning of the Industrial Revolution, people had been allotting God less and less of a role in their daily lives. Churchgoing had gradually dropped off or been perfunctorily confined to the most special holy days. What Christian ministers grumblingly call "Christmas Christians" applied to people of every faith. Throughout the reign of "science as religion," that drifting away had continued until, ten years ago, surveys in America showed that the percentage of registered church members regularly attending church was at an all-time low. In other industrialized countries, the situation was much the same.

Now the preachers again raised their voices, and some of them proclaimed the shocking words, "God is dead!" They said that God had become meaningless to most people, unnecessary for guidance and uninspiring as a force for betterment. Of course, the preachers did not mean to encourage this trend—they hoped to reverse it—but the "God is dead" catch phrase was taken literally by a large number of people, and "God is dead" was repeated in cocktail party conversations, in slick magazines and in newspapers, as if it was really true and had just been discovered.

Every "new" intellectual theory is always taken up by the people of its time as if it were original with them, and proof of their being able to think more intelligently than their forebears. In fact, the "God is dead" notion, or notions very like it, had been voiced time and again through the centuries, even by extremely backward and unintellectual peoples.

Many primitive societies have believed in what anthropologists call "the otiose creator." (*Otiose* is just a fancy word for "idle.") Such societies conceded that there was a God, and that he created everything that exists, but then, they said, he found the workings of the universe too trivial to interest him, and so went off to snooze or loaf somewhere, leaving the details of the universe's workings to the supervision of insignificant and inefficient nature spirits.

The European Freethinkers of some 300 years ago believed in an absentee God who had set the universe going—like winding up a clock—and had then departed to let it work out its own evolution, its problems and, if possible, its own perfection.

Philosopher Miguel de Unamuno, fifty years ago, propounded the theory that God is and always has been *asleep.* The universe and everything in it is merely a dream he is having. God is likely to awaken at any moment, and all his dream creatures—including you and me—will blink into oblivion just the way our own dream characters do when we wake up. (Unamuno further theorized that all the prayers men have uttered throughout history have been unconscious attempts to lull God into a deeper sleep, so he won't wake up and make us all disappear.)

These notions, whether of philosophers or of ignorant tribesmen, would be as good a way as any of accounting for all the things that go wrong, the persistence of war, wickedness and wretchedness in the world. But the majority of people, of whatever faith, even if they wander away for a while, rally again to the God or gods they have long adored—and such people are not inclined to think of their deities as uncaring clock-winders, or idle, or asleep. True, the boons bestowed by early science and the banes threatened by modern science caused a number of people to look on religion as outmoded, but only for a time. After that "God is dead" low point of a few years ago, the worldwide resurgence of belief in God—or in some god—has been little short of spectacular.

This has been especially marked in the United States (the most science-minded of societies), and particularly noticeable among its young people. A recent survey in the United States showed that twice as many adults are regularly attending religious services as there were ten years ago. Another poll, of people under thirty years of age in nine of the world's leading nations, revealed that young Americans go to church oftener than those in any of the other countries surveyed. More than one in three attend at least weekend services in their church or temple, and many attend weekday services as well.

Besides those who have turned (or returned) to the long established religions of the West, some four million Americans and millions among other nationalities have taken up Buddhism,

Taoism and other Eastern religions or philosophies. Some of these converts feel that the Western religions are too overburdened with trappings of doctrine, ritual and rules to be really helpful in giving them spiritual uplift. However, there are many who embrace the Eastern beliefs simply because those beliefs come from far away and are ages old; therefore they are mystic (often to the point of incomprehensibility); therefore they must conceal wisdom and secrets unknown to the West.

For some years now, the practice of Hindu Yoga has been popular in the Western world. Since it has been mainly confined to young people who flaunt it as a protest against their elders' humdrum religions—and to aging ladies who hope its physical exercises will keep them slim, unwrinkled and attractive—most other people have regarded it as no more than a fad.

In June of 1975, in Michigan, a 29-year-old yogi (practitioner of Yoga), told friends he was going to try "astral projection"—that is, send his soul voyaging apart from his body, one of the abilities long claimed by Indian yogis. In his room, he assumed the proper position and went into a trance. A couple of days later, still in that "mystic" position, he was found dead.

The occurrence was reported in newspapers all over the world, and believers were delighted—not, of course, at the fellow's death—but because here, at last, was public proof that Yoga could accomplish *something*. The man had projected his soul out of this world. A member of the Integral Yoga Institute, who called himself Dhamapati, immediately and solemnly explained to reporters that the death must be blamed on the fact that the deceased had been a yogi for only two years. "He must have been very inexperienced in astral projection," said Dhamapati. "He obviously did not know how to come back."

Other gurus and yogis likewise leaped into the limelight, to air their own opinions on why the man's soul was still roaming—though all were pleased to point to this incident as proof that astral projection was a "fact" which should silence those who had for so long sneered at Yoga. In the meantime, however, doctors had performed an autopsy on the unfortunate fellow's body. They reported that he had been a drug user, and that their tests showed he had died of an overdose of cocaine. This sensational "case of the lost soul" faded from the newspapers, and the Yoga experts faded into embarrassed silence.

Other "philosophies and religions" have lately come out of the allegedly wise, mystic and secret East. I set them in quotation marks because—even though they may bring spiritual, mental or even physical benefits to some of their practitioners—to their founders they are money-making propositions. The best known of these practices is Transcendental Meditation, a simple series of mental exercises borrowed from Yoga which has made its founder, Maharishi Mahesh Yogi, a wealthy man. He seldom makes an appearance in public any more, and even less often does he do any teaching. That is left to his "disciples," graduates of his course, who go far and wide to start new TM Centers, enroll new members and split their fees with the Maharishi.

Another new fad out of India is the Divine Light Mission, of which the teen-aged Maharaj-Ji is the Perfect Master. Or he is at this writing. The young Master is fighting dethronement by his own mother and brother, who claim he has dimmed the Divine Light and want to take the leadership out of his hands. Anybody might yearn to succeed the Maharaj-Ji. Though he preaches simple, communal living, the eating of vegetarian meals, and the avoidance of sex, drugs and alcohol, the Maharaj-Ji lives as he pleases, in privacy, on any one of three American estates, has his choice of riding in one of his chauffeured limousines or in either of two private jet planes, and—to the horror of Divine Light followers in India—he has married a non-Indian (American) girl.

The United Family, claiming a membership of 500,000 in the United States alone—few of these are over thirty years old—is the creation of a South Korean "doctor," Sun Myung Moon. Moon stresses that his followers should make a good marriage, produce lots of children, and concentrate on family togetherness. Every few years, Moon arranges a mass-wedding ceremony somewhere in the world, and hundreds or thousands of young couples travel there to be married. Moon preaches that out of the United Family will someday come a Christlike new Messiah to save the world—and Moon is not bashful when his followers tend to regard him as that Messiah. Meanwhile, he owns three valuable tracts of property in New York, one of which, his personal home, is a vast and deluxe river-view mansion.

It is easy to find fault with the old established faiths and to turn to something either much more obscure or brand new, but at least the old faiths were founded by men who never asked a penny for their teachings and who did not live playboy lives at the expense of their followers. Too many confused and gullible people today are willing to pay any price for "the truth" and "fulfillment," as if either could be bought and swallowed entire, like an instant-soul-vitamin pill. Nourishment of the soul is a lifelong job, and not even the holiest of mortals has ever claimed to have achieved either absolute truth or total fulfillment here on earth.

Let's get back to the more accepted gods and their more enduring faiths. According to the latest available estimates, about 2,600,000,000 people in the world belong to one of the major organized religions, from Roman Catholics (the most numerous) to Zoroastrians (the fewest). But there are many other religious groups too isolated or too small to be accurately counted. Let us make a guess at another 500 million members for all of them together. Then let's guess at perhaps another 50 million people who temporarily belong to one of those fad religions—though we might consider them drifters in search of a faith, who will probably settle eventually into some established religion. Add all those figures and we are left with some 600 million people in the world who apparently do not practice any religion or believe in any god at all. This is not necessarily so.

Of course, there are the atheists, who flatly deny the existence of any god, creator, afterlife or any other aspect of religious belief. Indeed, in those countries governed by Marxist communism, religion is regarded much as we regard drug-taking, and atheism is the only acceptable belief (if total disbelief can be called that). However, it is well known that some people in Communist countries disregard this official attitude, and do practice secretly some form of god worship.

And there are agnostics, who neither believe nor disbelieve in God, Heaven, Hell, and so on, but say simply "show me." They are perfectly willing to believe in a deity if his or her existence can be proven. Also, many agnostics will concede that they don't believe, either, that the universe "just happened." Most will grant that this intricate, interconnected scheme of everything from galaxies to subatomic particles was the doing of some Higher Power beyond their understanding.

However, atheists and agnostics cannot possibly account for all of those 600 million people in the world who, by our estimates and guesses, apparently practice no religion and worship no god whatsoever. Most of those millions must be men and women who simply choose not to affiliate themselves with any organized church, but instead worship their own concept of God (or gods) in their own private way.

For those who choose, on their own, to deny the existence of God or any other gods, novelist Robertson Davies has probably made the best retort. To a character in one of his novels who confesses he is an atheist, another character says, "I'm not surprised. You created a God in your own image, and when you found out he was no good you abolished him."

L'ENVOI

No, the heart that has truly loved never forgets,
But as truly loves on to the close;
As the sunflower turns on her god, when he sets,
The same look which she turned when he rose.

— THOMAS MOORE

INDEX

OF

NAMES